The Ordinary Mind

A Soul Adventure by Rod Hunt

Earth Cosmos Press

A CIP catalogue for this book is available from the National Library, Ireland, and the British Library.

ISBN: 978-0-9712693-5-1
1. Religion & Spirituality. 2. Buddhism. 3. Autobiography.

Cover design by Harper Stone.

Published by:
Earth Cosmos Press, Ireland.
www.EarthCosmosPress.org

Contacting the Author:
cairapress@arvig.net

CONTENTS

The Ordinary Mind

Sᴇᴍ ɪs ᴀ Tɪʙᴇᴛᴀɴ ᴡᴏʀᴅ for the ordinary mind. One Master, Chogyam Trungpa, describes it as being, "That which possesses a sense of duality – which grasps or rejects something external – that is the mind. Fundamentally it is that which can associate with an 'other' – with any 'something' that is perceived as different from the perceiver."

It is the thinking mind which cannot operate unless it is in relation to a projected and falsely seen outer point of reference.

One can assume from this that it is the mind that thinks: It can manipulate external situations, it harbors desires, explodes in anger, generates negativity and in order to continue its activities, and it produces conditioning elements to validate its own falseness. It is self protecting, cunning, skeptical and deceptive in its self preservation. It rationalizes, develops chaos within, confusion sickness and death without hope.

Hidden within sem is the very nature of the mind, an essence untouched by change and death and until freed, is clouded and waiting.

In *The Tibetan Book of Great Liberation* by W.Y. Evens-Wentz, Donald Lopez, Jr. explains the thought process of SEM: the Ordinary Mind. He says, "Because it is undistinguishable, ordinary and remains where it is, the clear and lucid knowing is called, "the ordinary mind." No matter what auspicious and poetic names are used, it is, in fact, nothing other than the, *sic* our, personal awareness. Whoever wants more is like someone searching for the elephant's tracks when the elephant has been found."

Oh dear, oh dear! We must look into this!

Rod Hunt
Kinsale, County Cork
IRELAND 2004-2010

Author's Notes

C.G. Jung has said that the modern interpretation of the mind has switched from something metaphysical to being a psychic function. It has no connection with the primordial oneness of the concept of a Universal Mind. In other words, there is no physiological data proving that the mind can exert itself beyond its own properties.

We are still, however, led to believe or told to put our faith in something that cannot be happen, i.e., know God. Thus science, on basis of fact, opposes religion in that aspect.

We tend to "think" of the mind as an arbitrary thing, but the truth is that every reality is a psychic image and nothing exists unless we are able to mentally see it. We are obsessed with conditions of factual structure and the danger is that unless we learn to think we accept what others say and that becomes our internalized perception.

In the East, the mind is cosmic and so there is no conflict between religion and science. As C.G. Jung explains it, "There is no conflict between religion and science in the East because no science is there based upon the passion for facts, and no religion upon mere faith."

There is a connection with that in these stories and at times I found that my processing of the experiences related herein rested somewhere in between the western and the cosmic. The origin of some of the stories presented is in involuntary recollection or flashbacks, dream–like states of consciousness and near trance conditions. The others come from personal convictions.

EPISODE 1:

RETREAT TO IRELAND

Truth is sometimes stranger than fiction.

DZOGCHEN BEARA SPIRITUAL CENTRE
GARRANES, CASTLETOWNEBEARA
COUNTY CORK, IRELAND
                    NOVEMBER, 2004

THE POPE IS DYING. My wife has died. I'm sick with grief. Too many are angry and I know why. My adopted country of Ireland is giving me some anxiety as it appears to be going from good to getting worse.

MY MIND IS UNSETTLED, as always, it seems. It's supposed to rest in pure awareness if I'm doing the meditation correctly, but that's been increasingly hard to do of late. Everything in my life has been so wild and I'm distracted by both the memory of past events and my new and totally unfamiliar surroundings at Dzogchen Beara.

I am not really certain of the reasons for my being here.

I have some experience with the teachings; that I am to bring together the essential nature of my mind so I understand my own shifting moods and how they can be calmed. There is a Tibetan saying, "Gompa m yin kompa yin," which, I am told, translates that mediation is nothing more than getting used to the actual practice of mediation. So, that being true, it's not something I can force, but rather it has to happen spontaneously and that can only happen when I've perfected the practice.

I live in hope.

My teacher tells me an unsettled mind such as mine is at present as a candle flame, unstable, flickering, constantly in change, fanned by the strong, violent winds of my thoughts and emotions. This is Sem, the ordinary mind, and hidden within it is the very nature of the mind – an essence untouched by the change and death and, until freed, is clouded and waiting. It can only burn at the desired steadiness if the air around it is made still so I can begin to find the natural peaceful nature.

He warns me, too, that as a westerner I'll be further distracted by the technical training I've grown up in. He said, "endured" rather than "grown up" and I believe he is correct in his interpretation. In other words, I am to try to obliviate that background noise of analyzing every thought. That isn't the technique of meditation, but rather the spirit.

I am thinking, "Yeah, sure."

As the meditation session starts I am remembering my

experiences of long ago when I tried, with a modicum of success I must say, Transcendental Meditation. I could do that blanking of the mind business and I had my personal mantra that wasn't distracting and that helped concentration. That was the stuff of amateurs and I now know that the blanking of the mind was really quite futile. It simply cannot be done effectively, at least not by me.

This now, however, is not that, though there is to be the same attention to assuming the correct posture. I am sitting as though I am a mountain, though I'm certain I lack the majesty and steadfast make-up of Mt. McKinley or Fuji, which are within my personal past. My back, which has its own problems to begin with, is to be "like a stack of gold coins." The straight back keeps me awake and lets the "prana" or inner energy flow easily through the subtle channels of my already questioning body.

My legs are now crossed as I sit on my piece of carpet, my head is balanced on my neck and I'm starting with my eyes closed, though I'm told it's better to keep them open and in a gazing state, which is a relaxed, unwavering stare.

I'm already beginning to feel the tension leaving, not in a sleepy mode, but I'm not focusing on anything. I am, however, distracted by my wandering thoughts. I "push them away" and feel the descending mood of peace, though I am surrounded by 30 others in a silent cocoon of mutuality. I am warmed by their company and I open my eyes, resting the focus in a space in mid-air directly in front of me. I'm looking down my nose. There is a quiet emptiness that surrounds me in a feeling of compassion and equanimity.

Be well, be happy, be safe.

Time is gone. As I drift, as I gently disregard the waves

of thought, all seems well for unknown moments. Then instead of light there is darkness and the image of a pale, haunted, pained face appears. There is no escape, no gentle force for disregard or turning away. I am trembling and alert, fully aware of my last sight of my wife as she died that humid and threatening morning in the hospice.

Is this what I came for? Is this what I will face in practice and not coming to understand the inevitability of dying and death?

Every thing is nothing. Only what you can carry through the passage between life and death is of consequence. Death has no meaning to love. Truth survives all ensuing encounters, whatever their nature.

I have no wish to discuss this with my teacher, but he already knows I've lost the substance.

"What happened to you this evening?" he asks.

"Nothing. I just have a hard time in practice. I'll be fine."

"If you have questions, just ask them. Perhaps we can help. The first encounters are the hardest, believe me," he said, smiling and giving me the look that said he recognized my fear.

These people know. They can read me and I shouldn't ignore that if I really want to learn why I'm here. Later, two other attendees sharing Cottage #3 with me are staring at the ocean 100 feet away, 100 feet down. The evening tide is in and the Atlantic is rolling and crashing onto the rocks below. We are pledged to silence when all of us would sooner talk. I want to share my thoughts and experiences of the afternoon's and evening's mediation periods. Instead, we incubate and turn our moods inward. They are nothing, too.

I cannot and care not to stop my thoughts of my beloved wife as they affect me. Am I who I am now? If not, who was I before this happened? It is dizzying as I wander in the life after death. At what age are we then and are we reunited with our parents and are they reunited with theirs and does the process go on until we are all reunited with the very first family on earth? And before that, what? In my wife's mind-life and in her slow and debilitating death, would she be reincarnated as she was at the time of her passing, or would she be reincarnated as she was at her mental and thus, her physical best? There are no bodies out there. Buddha was the Enlightened One and he knew everything.

Padmasambhava, the Great Guru, was banished to the charnel grounds after accidentally killing the son of one of the king's favorite ministers. There he made his clothes from the shrouds the dead were wrapped in and ate the food left for them, but when the famines came and there were no more shrouds or food offerings, he ate the flesh of the dead and dressed in clothes made of the skin of the dead, so he really understood those practicalities.

No one can tell me, but the directions on learning the practice are clear. Stay focused. Meditate. Read. Listen to the chants of Lama Tashi as the Master's deep tones take the world to the basics through purification, enlightenment, compassion, wisdom, power, long life, protection and healing. And, I read the dedication of merit:

> Through this merit, may all beings attain
> the omniscient state of enlightenment
> And conquer the enemy

of faults and delusions.
May they be liberated from the ocean
And from its pounding waves of
birth, old age, sickness and death.

I don't understand the origin of thoughts as being independent of the mind and the mind's many natural chemical reactions. How am I to come to meditation with such initial purity as to avoid normal human reactions? Fasting produces altered states of awareness and conscience. A person who has fasted for several days is often subject to hallucination and the chemical reaction to starvation is "abnormal' in as much as the chemical electrolyte constant of the body is distorted. I think the mind and body of an 18 year old is dramatically different than a person of my age and years of medication or abuse. Surely, that will alter the mental make up, our basic metabolism changes and so forth. How can those factors not be an influence on the approach to meditation? Can those who are meditating regularly control that, and they surely must be able to overcome the inconsistencies by calming the mind. If I can't do that, or if my mind stays in complex combat with calming, what will happen? Is there a side step into trance?

Last night, before I slept, I was reading one of John O'Donohue's books; the one on beauty. What I should be has to do with my missing spirituality. I'm staggered by reading Buddhist beliefs and I am overwhelmed by the fact that most of what I'm reading about beauty is conceptually what I already knew and maybe others who read O'Donohue's many layered materials think so, too. They love him because he sermonizes on what they know, but haven't mentally captured before. He makes it easy.

The most disturbing thing about this whole adventure into beauty is that I can read it and understand it, but I can no longer remember it for more than five minutes. Does this mean that his writing is what Torbert's informational theory calls "noise"? I know a lot about that, but I can no longer articulate it. It isn't worth the rehearsal. If somebody asked me about the concept of beauty as an essential of life, I couldn't tell them anything meaningful and that's bothersome because not long ago I could produce the words. Since Norma died, I can't. Is there a connection between her death and beauty that has now so reduced the issue? Is it something that will come back? I sincerely doubt it, and I no longer care as it isn't worth the effort of concentration. Is it natural that all beauty withers and dies within us?

I'm stirred to consciousness as there is movement and sound and coffee. There are 20 minutes until the morning session and when the enduring practices in the shrine room are to start. It is raining desperately and the wind is strong, coming off the Atlantic below in alarming gusts that push me sideways and backward as I climb the path to join the others. We are still in silence and try to avoid eye contact.

I'm seated, or more accurately, in the lotus position, as instructions to assist meditation begin. There are those present who are new to practice and the fundamentals are reviewed. Back straight, normal breathing, eyes looking into space at 45 degrees in front. We are looking inward and not chasing thoughts or projections. The mind is what we are looking into and we are seeking the truth, not outside, but within the nature of the mind. To be able to do so will free us from the fear of death and will help us to realize the truth of life. We are reminded that if we are too clever, we could miss the point entirely. It is said that the logical mind seems interesting, but it is the seed of delusion. We are charged with bringing the mind home.

The review includes the suggestion of the use of an object, such as a picture of Buddha or Padmasambhava to help our meditation. I think of the beautiful head of Padmasambhava, crafted and fired by the 14 year old son of a former student who made it for me just because I once had mentioned how helpful it would be for me. Would that everyone could be as thoughtful and kind!

Also mentioned in the preparatory remarks is the Tibetan technique of the mantra. It is OM AH HUM VAJRA GURU PADMA SIDDHI HUM, and it carries the blessing of the 12 types of teaching taught by Buddha. This is the very essence of the 84,000 Dharmas and by the recitation of those 12 syllables of the Vajra Guru mantra through the 12 links you are purifying yourself. It is remarkably powerful, as I can surely attest.

We are now advised to watch the breath. The mouth is slightly open and the tongue is resting on the palate. For some physiological reason, the mouth does not become distractingly dry if this process is used. We are reminded to focus on the out-breath. Osho, the 20th century Indian mystic was a follower of Atisha and his breathing practice was so intense he was convinced that his in-breath was meant to pull all the evils of the world within him and he consumed them; his out-breath then being pure.

I am distracted by the thought that one is to forego ego in all its many and crippling forms. This being true, I am questioning how one can compromise one's ego while thinking one can breathe in all the evils of the world and digest them? Is this the purity of the soul or is it an affectation of one's search for power; his ego? With Atisha I must believe it is the former. He was so successful in cutting himself off that he believed "I am not." The person is absent, and that in his own total consciousness he is God and so is everyone else.

That's an overwhelmingly powerful conviction and not one likely to be enormously popular with western world Christians. I wonder to myself if there are now any Christians who qualify as thinkers in the same league with those of the East?

As I bring myself back to the three methods of meditative enhancement I am assured each of the three forms a complete meditation practice. Each one appeals to the individual's particular modality; the breathing being the closest to tactile because you actually do feel it and if you begin to feel it like Atisha, and probably Atisha's master, Dharmakirti, you've probably added an absolute to the practice known only to those in the most revered meditative circles. I don't think I can go there, but I will try to do my best to at least enter that unconscious mind-free state.

The object is the sight modality and the chanting of mantras or hearing them is auditory and that, then takes in the three cognitive learning processes. All this long, long before anyone invented the teaching cycles used since Socrates and Plato. What is even more amazing about the meditation practice is that the masters have never, ever, down through the centuries, entered into the mystery-mastery complex process, whereby if you know something or possess something, you keep it from others to give yourself leverage; not to mention that ego-enhancing feeling that you're better.

Here, they share with great pleasure all that you can absorb of their knowledge as the gift of enlightenment.

Logically, once one becomes accomplished at entering the higher meditative state one will no longer need the watching of the breath, the object or the chant. One can then dispossess them, just as one would dispossess one's worldly belongings and ego. It is as though one had a boat to cross the river to reach the mountain one must climb, whatever that mountain happens to be, and one shoves the boat back. No one needs a boat to climb a mountain.

As the instructor continues, we will go into practice, using about 25 per cent of our mind to watch our breathing out. For those of us who have been practicing meditation, we can advance ourselves by applying another 25 per cent of our minds to watching ourselves watching our breath. This is called "Peaceful Remaining," or "Calm Abiding," and it diffuses our negativity. What we are to find first is to feel well in our own being, which will, in turn as time goes on, dissolve the unkindness or harmfulness within ourselves.

So, one brings the mind home from all our troubles and problems and one will be relaxed. Again, be well, be happy.

The great living teacher, Sogyal Rinpoche tells us that when he meditates, he is inspired by a poem by Nyoshul Khenipothat which urges us to:

Rest in the natural great peace
This exhausted mind
Beaten helpless by harm and neurotic thought,
Like the relentless fury of the pounding waves
In the infinite ocean of samsara

The goal of this practice and the objective of all of us who are present is to find peace or find oneself in self resting, or nowness. This is the Calm Abiding and our teacher compares the mind to a glass of muddy water. If you don't stir it, it will become clear. The mud is still there and likely to be stirred again, but we now know how to cause it to settle. Bringing the mind home does that.

This doesn't lead us to enlightenment or liberation because as long as we remain in the domain of the subject-object duality, we are still ignorant.

The process has started and I'm not yet overwhelmed because I've been practicing for a while; two years to give it a frame. It is, nevertheless, a huge concept so foreign to most western minds that when the teacher told us that we will now meditate, I was certain my mind would be in such an active state that there wasn't a chance I'd be able to calm down. The gong, which is a little brass bowl, is struck by the teacher to signify the beginning of the session of practice. That sound alone is enough to start the calming and while still buzzing I begin to watch my breath. I am looking at a huge picture of a statue of Padmasambhava on the side wall of the shrine and I chant to myself my abbreviated mantra, OM MANI PADME HUM, the mantra of compassion, the mantra given by Avalokiteshvasa to Buddha.

I am using all three methods and it is enormously effective. Everything disappears. I have no concept of how long it took to get to this state of near nothingness, but all is serene and I am seeing a beam, just a tiny beam of red light entering my body from Padmasambhava's eyes.

I should be startled, but I am not. I am simply watching with the mind's eye, not my eyes, as the beam slowly reaches me and enters at about the sternum. It is personal and I don't have any thought about it; so much just meant to be. I don't wonder if this is to be expected or whether I am entering a trance-like state. I'm not frightened nor am I bewildered.

The gong sounds again to return us. We are still in silence and I wouldn't have spoken of it to anyone other than my teacher, but I don't have any reason to do so. Somehow, I'm sure he already knows.

In that silence there is a true bonding of fellowship. In World War II on board the tiny landing ship which was my combat-encased home for nearly two years in the southwest Pacific there would be a fear induced silence. Always, during those silences I felt a strong sense of companionship and of team belonging. Actually, if you weren't a religious person, that camaraderie was all you had to hang on to, other than those tiny strong threads, the letters from home.

This was very different. As I looked around the shrine room there was not one single person for whom I did not feel the strength of love. And, I didn't wonder if it was mutual because it no longer mattered. I knew there was an absolutely wonderful new dimension to my consciousness; my awareness.

All this could change if I stirred the water.

EPISODE 2:

AN IRISH VISITOR

O N THE NEXT DAY, after a deep sleep unlike any I've had in four years, I am now somewhat apprehensive; even a bit frightened. Is what I experienced the day before something I want to revisit, this unexplainable light emanating from Padmasambhava? Is this normal in the state of Calm Abiding? Even if it is, and I surely doubt it, am I able to again achieve that level of nowness? Can one drop over that edge? What is it that lies beyond that that could possibly be of meaning or interest to me other than a morbid fascination I have always felt for the other side of life? Am I brave enough to handle it with calm if I am able to reproduce the state of other-worldliness? I am in a guilt-state because I had other objectives when I came here which had nothing to do with what I now face. Am I using an ancient practice of meditation for false reasons or is it simply that I am able to stand at the window and look into... into what? This is only the third day of the Rigpa sessions and I have already, in my own mind, violated the purpose of the teachings.

Perhaps it will not visit again and I will no longer go into the hypnogogic state of yesterday ever again. Perhaps I will be better able to steer myself into the Calm Abiding and forego the enraptured world of some past or unknown life of either myself or whomever I am representing. The more I think of it, the more certain I become that it is necessary to proceed with whatever I am given, though I certainly don't look upon it as a special ability. I don't know anything about it actually, so it isn't something I can control other than not putting myself into the situation again if I want or need to avoid it. And, what if this is now beyond control and I am taken into the void of the unknown, even in sleep? What happens and how does one awaken oneself if that condition occurs and is persistent or if it can take possession of the conscious mind as well?

My mother would have simply said I was, "in a pickle."

She would also have said I should not question my courage, but rather proceed with conviction.

And, so I shall.

The shrine is open at all times and even though it is getting late I pull on my foul weather gear and start, not for the shrine, but for the stupa along the path to the ocean cove below. It is a miserable night and I don't know why I am going to the stupa instead of the shrine. I simply follow my instincts and start walking. Along the way I meet a dark line of people led by one of the instructors, all with eyes down and singing in a low-voiced chant some mantra I am not familiar with. I realize these are disciples in training here and as such are far in advance of anything I know about their rituals, habits and their daily lives. I do know enough not to speak to them or to even try to look directly at them. They have such a quiet and unassuming manner as they walk slowly in their deep meditation. If there is holiness in western Buddhism, these are its representatives. They pass by me as I step off the path and turn away toward the hillside, looking for the burning lamp of the stupa.

Again I am taken by the thought that whatever it is that I am about to enter into with myself, I should think seriously about it because I continue to have this gnawing feeling that what I am contemplating is wrong and not in accordance with any Buddha doctrine, liberal and inviting of free thought as it is. My cause of wonderment is simple enough to understand. I have read hundreds of the stories of those whom I believe to be classified as arhats, or worthy ones who have realized nirvana by following the teachings of Buddha. Some of their experiences and others' experiences of the devas in their battles and struggles with the demonic and supernatural ashuras are, to me, quite honestly, unbelievable. Those heroic encounters are said to be real and not something created out of the imagination to frighten followers into staying on the correct paths. These are not the stories of aliens or even comparable to those told in the Holy Bible of the living devil. There is an otherworld, vividly portrayed in their thousands by those who have experienced their horrors.

As I reach the stupa and sit before it, first circling it several times to establish the mood, I think of Yama, the Lord of Death, whose position in the centre of the Tibetan Wheel of Life is meant to remind us of the tendency of human beings to cling to material existence.

That Wheel of Life is, in its essence, a map of *samsara*, the cycle of constant rebirth we are all trapped in as a result of our constant misdeeds. Yama claims the dead and oversees the karmic retribution, so he is as ever present as an enforcer. If I am to believe this, then there are many dangers ahead. I am an admitted carrier of the seeds of karma and as such I am, therefore, a possible subject to be reborn in the third realm and am probably thus classified as a form of demon. I am certainly not in either of the first two realms of being. I have no grand aspirations of achieving Nirvana, nor am I now, nor will I ever be reborn as a deva, for as the Christians say, "I have sinned mortally" and I should add, intentionally. I don't even want to think of the other three realms, principally because I think I have suffered enough without understanding any of the possible reasons why, other than my own ignorance.

They are threatening, though, and again, if I am to believe any or all of this, they could make me devoted to better moral behavior. That's if I live through this next set of episodic encounters I feel I must face. If I start seeing the kleshas, those three animals in the Wheel, I know I must back off; or more likely, cut and run, never to enter into the worlds I think I am about to view. I am not a coward, but I am certainly not going to act stupidly in the presence of the unknown.

This experience that I am about to attempt to undergo has nothing to do with escaping from *samsara* through spiritual means. The four Noble Truths are just that and I understand that, too. This is separate and independent of any of the truly noble and magnificent purposes espoused in the teachings of Buddha. I must make this clear in my own mind to convince myself that I am not trying to make use of what I have learned to explore something that has, really, nothing to do with the Dharma of the eternal moral order or eternal truth. What I am going to do is, essentially, irreligious, and though the mystics have glimpsed and practiced this for centuries, it is my own mental fusion, or maybe fission, and I must not cross over into any of the Buddhist teachings in order to rescue myself once this starts. They had nothing to do with it and I am guilty of taking their good works and making the decisions to enter into that part of the brain that is not the mind.

That, as I have also learned from Sogyal Rinpoche, has nothing to do with the bardo of becoming, where the mind becomes endowed with immense clarity. I am the lonely sailor on this sea, at least for the time being. I need to keep focused on the fact that this isn't meditation in the true sense. It only starts there and where I take it or it takes me is as opposite as can be imagined.

As I sit quietly facing the stupa and as I gaze at the light of the lamp I am becoming incredibly at ease. The idea of going to the shrine is slowly sinking into an obscure recession. I am there, not at all aware of the silence of the entire world, save the sea below in its constant rumbling and rolling over the rocks. I can see it without looking and the vision is one of enormity and power, but there is no threat – it simply encompasses all. I am not aware of the bliss. It is simply there and the narrator arrives. What my mind is telling me is that what I am about to experience is a trance-like recollection.

I am agreeable to this. Like the sea below, it washes over

me, wholly, completely and is totally believable.

The narrator is visible to me. He sits in a library-like room near a window and he wears a robe of the Benedictine Order. The hood covers his head and he is in such a position that I cannot actually see his face. There is an aura of quiet certainty surrounding him and in his hands there is a chronicle. He begins with a nod to me and he reads.

As old as Ireland, that is the age of conflict it has endured. The wars raged, the battles fought, the blood and the tears flowed incessantly and forever. The nobles of Ireland and their clans suffered and survived in any and every fashion imaginable, but primarily by absorbing the invaders and marrying them, thus making the race of the usurpers more intelligent. Little of this kind of fact is available in reverse for the dominant Irish genealogy.

Henry II had deemed it necessary to protect England by seizing Ireland from his vassal Strongbow to prevent him from winning independent power there. He obtained the infamous Bull of Adrian which authorized him to invade and restore the restive island to the Church. The Irish Catholic Church was compelled to submit to Rome at the Synod of Lismore. English law and the power of the Crown extended only in the Pale until the later reign of Edward II and his persistence in the subjection of the Irish Church to England caused the chiefs of Ulster to look abroad for a strong ruler. They selected Edward Bruce who landed in Antrim in 1315 with 6,000 Scots joining with the O'Neills.

The Crown attempted by the Statute of Kilkenny (1367) to draw the Normans and English away from the Irishry, but by then it was too late. They had already adopted the language and the laws of the land they had conquered to MacCarthy Reagh, and then to the O'Donnells of Donegal.

When Henry VIII broke with the Pope, the influence of the Church was thrown against him. England's many enemies looked to Ireland as a staging area and a solid ally. To Henry, Ireland became the salient in the English defense and had to be held. Henry planned to hold Ireland through the great lords and he conferred titles on O'Neill, O'Donnell, O'Brien and Burke. Because of the religious cleavage, the plan could never be successful.

The alternative was the plantation with Englishmen to be cultivators in peace and the king's soldiers in the inevitable wars to follow.

Henry VIII's grant of English titles did create dissension in every clan and England carried out her plan of 'Divide et impera.' Elizabeth set up a queen's O'Reilly or a queen's O'Rourke, and split the power of every clan and when the rivals had reduced themselves to impotence, the Crown annexed.

Next to be broken was the Southern Geraldines under Gerald, the 15th Earl of Desmond. A fanatic, he obtained an army from Spain which landed at Smerwick. They surrendered to Grey on promise of safe passage home. All of them were infamously put to the sword.

By imprisoning Hugh O'Donnell in Dublin Castle the Crown was able to control the North of Ireland and the West of Scotland, but then the young fellow escaped over the Dublin Mountains. He grew to manhood and allied himself with O'Neill and the Northern League. The League was successful when O'Neill defeated Bagenal at

Yellow Ford near Armagh.

The Northern Lords knew the time had come to join with the Southern Catholic Army under the 16th Earl of Desmond, Sugaun and to march to Munster.

There entered then another powerful figure into the equation of struggle. Florence MacCarthy, the tanist of that Sept had been "a guest of Her Matie" in the Tower of London since he had committed a crime against the Queen by marrying Ellen, the daughter of the Earl Clancar, The MacCarthy Mor, without Her permission. Elizabeth sent him to Ireland to put down his hated brother-in-law and claimant to the title of Mor, Clancar's bastard son, Donal. The Queen also instructed him to collect the £500 Lord Barry owed her and to use it to equip an army to do her will whilst he was there. Florence was delighted.

Though the deeds of O'Neill and O'Donnell were many and famous, it was the popularity of Donal MacCarthy, Florence's rival and enemy, who captured the minds of Munster. He was an outlaw for having escaped Dublin Castle where he had been held as surety against his father's further mischief. Then he killed an Englishman who need-ed killing and he became "The Robin Hood of Munster." O'Neill would need them both in his service if he was to succeed in his Christian mission, but he was not going to get them both. There was too much bad blood between them and too much at stake in the gaining of the title of MacCarthy Mor. The Queen knew she had trouble, but O'Neill knew nothing of which way the tree would fall: with Florence it was his standing army of 5,000 and with Donal it was his tremendous popularity, but presently he commanded only 500 loose swords.

There were other causes than the impatience of his immediate neighbors that threatened to disturb the quiet that Florence desired to establish about him. In the meanwhile O'Neill's truces still continued, but, like fragile ice, dangerous to trust, and with incessant recurrence of ominous and alarming rumblings below their surface. Winter was at hand.

The truces afforded time for the English still in Ireland to complain about their lack of protection and for O'Neill to spend his time preparing for his excursion into Munster. He sent letters in regal style and pretension to the MacCarthy Muskerry, to Lord Roche, the Lord Barry, the white Knight, to the Earl of Desmond, and finally to Florence MacCarthy. "He would come to learn the intentions of the Gentlemen of Munster with regard to the great questions of the nation's liberty and religion."

O'Neill was as good as his word and in early January of 1600 he was marching and "the heart of every man in Munster beat exultantly when tidings of his first day's march reached them." Two Lord's, for very different reasons, were plunged into perplexity and alarm. The Lord Barry, the son of a rebel, born and trained in actual rebellion, had cast his lot with the Queen's government. For Barry, the coming of O'Neill was a sentence of destruction.

Ormond received the defiant letter from O'Neill stating his intentions to meet his friends at Holy Cross, or in polite language, "To confirm the determination of all the Traitors of Munster with new oaths, before that Idol, whom the Irish nation more superstitiously reverence than all the other idolatries in Ireland." Then, to the great dismay of the Lords of the Council, he determined to march with

5,000 men. In vain did these discreet men call to his re-
membrance the last meeting of the Queen's forces with
that formidable rebel. In vain did they plainly inform him
that "they desired not such another Journey as that of the
Blackwater."

Ormond was certain O'Neill would arrive at Holy Cross
inside his predicted time and he rushed his army toward
that point. "But the Lords Justices had no real cause for
their alarm; the speed of the royal troops had of late days
usually been in such direction as left safe distance between
them and the arch rebel."

O'Neill was on time to his trysting place. "He led his
force to the gate of the monastery of the Holy Cross, paused
there for the contentment of his devotion," and at his pleasure moved thence to Cashel, where he was joined by the
declared commander of the Southern Catholic Army, James
Fitz Thomas

From the moment O'Neill left Ulster he could be
tracked by the black, burned earth and trailed forward by
the smoke and flames. And these ruthlessly destroyed holdings were not those of his enemies. He was stating his
cause for Ireland and the Irish Catholic Church and not
necessarily the Catholic Church of Rome. It paused only
to destroy, and Barry watched as it drew daily closer to his
home. Barry still had ample time to choose for his coun-
trymen or to doom Barrycourt to the Queen. The Queen
had made his life miserable over the past ten years of his life
by, "the affronts put upon him in the matter of the Fyne,"
The unaccountable Barry chose the Queen!

And so, to O'Neill's camp came Florence along with every man of note of the clergy and nobility. They were there

to swear fealty and dedication to the freedom of Ireland through their support to the Great O'Neill. And it was there that Donal McCarthy, who had previously declared himself MacCarthy Mor, with the consent of O'Neill, was deposed from that dignity and Florence was selected by O'Neill, "with the consent of the church and the nobility" to be awarded the White Rod of Office by the Lord O'Sullivan Beare and Bantry.

Florence's decision was taken and the news was instantly carried to Power and Warham St. Leger and consequently to England.

O'Neill's path of destruction, as he had promised, grew wider and deeper along with the despair of the remaining English planters. The desolation was so great that Ormond declared that not a plantation owner stayed to show his title to the Signories which the Queen's Letters Patent had conferred upon him! Lord Barry's holdings became the target of choice for O'Neill, and he designated Florence to carry out the unholy task as a test of his loyalty and because he knew of the hatred that existed between the two.

Barry's loyalty left him "not a rick of corn, nor a hovel, of all his towns, unburnt,"

THE DARK FIGURE closes the book, turns, and looks at me.

I think, "Am I permitted to speak?"

The figure replies, "Yes, you may speak. I am certain there are questions."

"What was that all about?"

"That was a rehearsal. You are, after all, in Ireland."

"Is that all there is?"

"Oh, no! Absolutely not. It gets much, much worse, or

I should say it could get much worse. And, it could get better. It's largely up to you. As I said, this is just a rehearsal. And, you will learn that the reply I gave you was fairly typical of Irish non-commitment."

"Are you to be my guide?"

"I most certainly hope not," he replies and there is darkness.

I am awake and again gazing at the flame and not the figure. I am now aware of the sounds around me. There is moonlight and the overcast skies have cleared, the rain has stopped and I look at my wrist watch. Less than thirty minutes have passed since my arrival at the threshold of the scene.

I am no longer alone as the procession of walking disciples again slowly passes between me and the cliffs of the Atlantic. The chant is louder and it takes the place of the sound of the waves.

I say aloud, "I had expected something worse."

"Pardon me?" says a voice belonging to someone I recognize as a fellow participant.

"Oh, sorry. Nothing. Nothing at all," I reply and walk back to my cottage in a daze of disappointment and bewilderment.

Had I escaped my own fears? In apprehension, I didn't think I had.

EPISODE 3:

THE FLOOD
DIMENSIONS

A LOVELY PATH from the cottage leads past the stupa and down toward the ocean. It traverses the sharp topography of the grassland suitable only for sheep and at my age it is a challenge just to stay upright as I descend toward the cove below a farmhouse on the brow of a headland. It is likely too small to be qualified as a headland, but it is a promontory of some size. In the distance, in a day of wondrous sunlight I think I can see Dursey Island, a place of infamy during the days following the Battle of Kinsale in 1601. It was there the women and children from the Beara Peninsula had fled as safe refuge. The British saw it differently and the refugees were slaughtered in the hundreds; some reportedly leaping from the cliffs to their death holding their children in their arms rather than be bayoneted by the blood-crazed soldiers.

Dunboy Castle had fallen and Donal O'Sullivan Beare had begun his march with a thousand survivors toward Leitrim and the possibility of rejoining Hugh O'Neill, Earl of Tyrone. They were pursued in numbers by the British forces under Wilmot and exchanges between the hunted and the hunters were frequent with red hot lead flying in anger and in anguish.

Reaching the Shannon River they were backed up against a nearly impossible situation. The usual ferrymen were under threat of the penalty of death if they helped O'Sullivan in the crossing, yet cross it they must if they were to escape. The alternative was a battle against even greater odds and that was unacceptable to Donal. The solution was to kill 11 of their horses, skin them, eat the flesh, cut the willows beside the river and build a boat 26 feet long and some eight or ten feet wide.

With this curragh-style vessel 30 armed men at a time were ferried across the Shannon and more than a dozen crossings were made, a miraculous achievement in itself, to say nothing of the battles and skirmishes between the 40 men of O'Sullivan's rearguard and Sheriff Donogh MacEagon's ill fated men. Perhaps justifiably, the royalist MacEagon was killed.

The recollection of this boat building and crossing of the Shannon has brought to mind the story of Noah and the Ark and its companion story from The Gilgamesh Epic. I have often wondered about the story of the flood. Did the Hebrews get the story for the Old Testament from the cuneiform inscriptions of Mesopotamia? There is a genetic relationship between the two. It is said Abraham came from Sumeria.

As a former student of the late Dr. David Free, the Biblical Archeologist, I have had a long and latent curiosity about the story of the flood, the deluge as revealed in the Gilgamesh Epic and that of Noah and the Ark.

As I attempted to learn more than one means of meditation I had come upon Osho's second Sutra in which all phenomena are like dreams and that phenomena means you see and experience everything in every way. He taught that to arrive at a state of transcendental consciousness is to find the truth and the truth is God and that God is nothing but which is. It is a most interesting and challenging philosophical process of reasoning.

Osho also claimed that Tibetan writings place Jesus in India for 18 years and when he returned to Jerusalem, he came back interpreting Buddha's teachings. Those teachings were diametrically opposed to Hebrew beliefs in God which leaned toward hate being used to defeat evil. Buddha said one shouldn't fall to the celestial daemons, that is to say, ego. To what extent ego has dominated religious leaders, not religion, is another point so very intriguing. With Dan Brown's writing of *The DaVinci Code* having made so many startling revelations concerning the origins of Christian thought and need for power, whether factual or tongue in cheek, I was curious as to what meditation; meditation of the concentrated teaching, could bring to me.

The Old Testament, in the thinking of many scholars, is an ancient fairy tale. To others it is dogma and yet to others a clever and straightforward document setting forth what the early Jews thought and felt was man as a permanently evil creature who needs to be led in the most forceful way possible. The language was the hereditary doctrine of enforcement. I really don't care about that.

Osho's advice was to find a time and a space to be unoccupied, to sit silently, watching what's inside you. That is now relatively easy for me to do and certainly my location has helped achieve a state of concentration. The difference between previous meditative states and this is the concentration required. It is total concentration on a single subject, so, instead of meditation I would disappear into the object of the meditation. In this process, if successful, one achieves a commitment to cut off all but a single subject of the meditation to the exclusion of all else. It is to become so watchful of the mind as to stop the mind from possessing you.

I am uncertain as to my own ability to form a concentration shell that will allow me to shut out the sound of the Atlantic, which again is suddenly in a very stormy mood. A person in my present state of wonderment and anxiety worries about many strange thoughts and one of mine seems to be examining the possibility that the tremendous force of the ocean is a message for me about the catastrophe.

The one which the Old Testament speaks in Genesis 6:3 is of the 120-year period of grace given that the earth's people must abide by God's laws or suffer the most severe consequences imaginable. In the Gilgamesh Epic, there was no thought of granting mankind the opportunity to repent. The planned destruction was a guarded secret that even the great divinity Ea didn't dare openly tell his favorite, Utnapishtim. What he did do was to cause Utnapishtim to dream of the consequences of the imminent flood. That is significant to me.

Perhaps I will learn as I sit on the millionth rock in this

exposed pasture and go into meditative practice. I am incredibly relaxed, which is something I didn't really expect, but have learned not to question. If it is still light, I don't know it. Mentally and physically I am in a state of darkness and silence.

Entering the mode of concentration by means of mind control discipline is both difficult and awkward. I must reverse the process of expelling thought while centralizing on this single subject. If it is true that the human mind is capable of infinite recall I will hopefully be able to do this.

I can truthfully say now that it was not as difficult or as challenging as I had feared, primarily, I think, because of my years of experience in analyzing human intelligence information. A problem I am immediately sensing, though, is the conflicting credibility of both flood stories. By assuming a neutral and noncommittal position I am able to dismiss the block. I go first to the Gilgamesh Epic and from Dr. Free's teaching I am able to recall the texts and still blend the Old Testament with it.

Recalling this incredible episode now, I am clearly able to recognize the voice as my own. It begins with Utnapishtim's dream.

In his dream, Utnapishtim asks Ea what he is to tell his fellow citizens when they ask why he is building and provisioning a boat? Ea says he is to tell them he must leave the city because the god Enlil hated him and he would be better to go to his lord Ea and live with him. Then Enlil would pour blessings upon them, beginning with rain of wheat on a stormy evening. This is a lie, of course, but if you're going to kill almost everyone, what purpose is there to actually tell the truth? Utnapishtim is to allay any

misgivings that his friends may feel by assuring them be-
forehand that the weather signs of the deluge are really the
signs of coming prosperity, not destruction.

A Sumerian name for the ark is spoken as a magurgur,
or "a very great boat." The literal term for "a great house,"
is ekallu, with many stories and compartments, but there
is no etymological connection between the name and the
Hebrew term for the ark.

Utnapishtim describes his vessel as seven stories high
and divided into nine sections or sixty three compartments
with a roof like that of, "the subterranean, as strong as the
earth." It has a door and at least one window. He tells of
pouring six shar of pitch into the pitch pot, and three shar
of asphalt and caulking the boat with the substance. The
word he uses for pitch is the same in Hebrew as in the Epic.
Utnapishtim tells that he used three shar of oil, one for the
water stopper and the other two he meant to stow away.
The ark is built in an exact cube, 200 ft in each side and
displacing 228,500 tons.

Noah's ark, as was explained, was of three stories and has
"many, many rooms, too numerous to recall in number."
It has a door in the side and an opening for light below the
roof, one cubit in height and running all around the ship.
It is a flat bottomed vessel, rectangular, square on both ends
and straight up on the sides. The length is three hundred
cubits, and its height is thirty cubits, or 450 feet long, 45
feet high and 75 feet wide, displacing 43,300 tons.

A new, unknown voice is heard, not mine, nor is it
anyone I recognize. Again, I don't know if I am able to
understand the ancient Hebrew and Sumerian languages or
if the voice is in English. It doesn't matter. It explains that

Utnapishtim put all his gold and silver aboard and whatever he had of "the seed of all living creatures and caused all his family and relations, the game of the fields, the beasts of the field, all the craftsmen and the boatman to go up into it." The craftsman, I'm told, are the learned men who were put aboard, "to record the beginning, the middle and end of all things," and to bury those writings in Sippar to preserve the divine revelations about the world's beginning and to transmit, "the arts and sciences, human culture and civilization to the post diluvium race." He also spoke of the birds; a dove, a swallow, and a raven to be released to determine to what degree the waters had fallen.

In Genesis, the cause of the flood is torrential rains and the eruption of subterranean waters and in the Sumerian account it is rainstorms (amaru), cloudburst and mighty winds with thunder, lightning, the breaking of dikes and reservoirs, all due to "the raging of Adad," the god of storm and rain, but I am seeing gigantic sea works from seismic disturbances in the Persian Gulf with stupendous masses of water rolling up the Tigrus-Euphrates Rivers.

Accordingly, the flood lasted one year and eleven days, making Noah 601 years old when he finally disembarked onto land once again, this being the period covered in the Priestly Code. In contrast, the Yahivistic Narrative holds to the forty days and forty nights documentation.

By account of the Sumerian writings, the whole flood or deluge spanned just seven days before Utnapishtim left his huge craft and nobody has said how long the deluge itself lasted. The gods of the wells and irrigation, those of the underworld, had all lent their power to the creation of the flood and its destruction, but lost control. Those gods, and

even Adad, can be seen cowering like dogs in their highest
heavens. Ishtar, the beautifully voiced lady of the gods is
heard to cry out, "In truth the olden times have turned to
clay, because I commanded evil in the assembly of the gods!
How could I command such evil: How could I command
such a war to destroy my people? It is I who bring forth my
people and like the spawn of fish they now fill the sea!"

Now, at the end, Utnapishtim looked out and sees all is
silent and all mankind has turned to clay, with only Mount
Nisir, the Mount of Salvation, above water. The boat has
drifted to the south of the lower Zab, near Pir Omar Gudrun
in the southwestern part of Armenia. All creatures of the
earth have successfully been destroyed.

In four Old Testament passages the word Ararat is mis-
takenly given as the landing position. The highest point is
Mount Massis, near Fake Van, 17,000 feet above sea level.
Both accounts, from Septuagint and the Gilgamesh Epic,
speak of the release of their birds to attempt to determine
if there is other land now above water. Both indicate the
raven succeeded whereas the doves and the swallows returned. Noah continues to release the doves each week for
three weeks before they fail to return, signifying they have
found land.

Utnapishtim tells of "sending forth everything to the
four winds," when the raven failed to return.

God then speaks to Noah, telling him after two months,
"Go forth of the ark, thou and thy wife, thy sons and the
wives of the sons with them. Bring forth every living thing
that is with thee."

There is now a summing up being told. The voice, my
voice of logic, reminds me that Utnapishtim had entered

the boat upon the instruction of a friendly deity. The biblical story is pervaded by the spirit of complete submission to the will of God and their complete dependence upon Him. The Babylonian version reveals self-determination and self-reliance.

Noah and Utnapishtim are seen to end their confinement in acts of worship. Utnapishtim offers a sacrifice, first building an altar and then burning fragrant materials. His purpose of the offering seems to be grounded in the fact that he escaped against the wishes and intentions of the assembly of gods who had decreed complete extermination of the human race. He had, therefore, very good reason to fear them, Enlil in particular, and the offering is in gratitude as well as of a propitiatory nature.

Noah has built the altar and the ascending essence of his offering is more tranquilization to appease the wrath of God, kindled by the sins of mankind. God receives this well, He now seeing it has the manifestation of deep gratitude.

Both heroes are blessed, Utnapishtim with land and a new start, and Noah, still not fully forgiven, with the blessing first given at the creation for him and his sons to multiply and to fill the earth and have the power of life and death over animals.

The two stories are independent, but it is not difficult to see them as one: one borrowing from the other. The Babylonian versions are reflected in Genesis, shown to date from the end of the third or the beginning of the second millennium BC. Hence it could be concluded the biblical account is based upon Babylonian material. In turn, the Babylonian is dependent on the Sumerian stories. The conclusions are based on the geographic and topographic nature of the land, lending more credence to the alluvial plains of Babylonian and wholly inapplicable to the mountainous country of Palestine.

I am not getting any ethical reason for the flood in the Gilgamesh epic, and it appears as a capricious exercise of the gods. I am seeing absolutely no moral ideals of gods who set such destiny before mankind. There is a flash of reason in the Biblical stories and they are that God was sorry he created man. I visualized, too, the Babylonian gods regret (other than Enlil) the destruction of man.

With that frail insight, the concentration effort falls away, and I am once again merely sitting on a rock in the middle of a herd of sheep, with darkening shadows around me and the heavens above blossoming in black foreboding.

As I slowly make my way back up the narrow, hillocky, path I have the time to reflect upon this recent trip into an unreasonable past. My first conclusion is that the Gilgamesh Epic is more Buddhist in interpretation than is that of the Bible story. Then again, it may be a conclusion responded to if I understood more about Christian mysticism.

Smiling to myself, I also reflect that those conclusions and 2 Euro could buy me a much needed cup of hot coffee at most Beara shops.

EPISODE 4:

REVISITING JOSEPHUS

IN MY PRESENT SET of confusing circumstances I am somewhere, I think, between vague uncertainty and perilous
doubt. I am no longer able to truthfully determine whether
these dreamlike sequences are of either a terribly unstable
person or someone far more advanced in an unknown area
than I really want to be. And I don't see any need to make a
determination either way because I intend to keep challenging the electrodes and take what I can get.

One of the many questions is whether or not these teachings of the masters as regards the abandonment of ego is being
violated or disregarded as I enter the arena of each experiential eventuality. It is difficult to discern where this necessary
discipline of concentration meditation falls. Is it producing
truth to banish ignorance or is it producing fully unfounded
fantasy?

I am not so much concerned about the smaller, everyday imperative truth of situations as I am about finding the truth of reality. The experiences I am having are hardly of the intellectual resonance to warrant worry. What I mean is I am not doing a search. I am only reacting to the mind vision of either previous personal happenings or historical knowledge. Whatever the case, I am certainly not shaking any foundations, but I am in a boundary free learning mode, both inside and outside; perhaps in a circular fashion, but learning nonetheless.

Still, the essential essence of the word "truth" is not really an issue and I feel free to continue in the dark cave of concentration on a single subject in hopes of learning something very new or relearning something forgotten. If all is nothing, I am well on the way. Are we living in a dream and are we asleep, even when we think we are awake? Will I, at some moment in altered being, achieve the *sannya* where the closing of the doors will allow leaving the mind outside my moment to moment existence in a void of that nothingness? Or will I continue to merely look through the windows of time and stay floating in a self-imposed void and not nothingness?

In the ethereal clone of last night's torrent of the flood I found an unexplained kinship, or more appropriately, a yearning, to see more of the Hebrew dilemma. Somehow, I was reminded of a conversation I had with a very bright young man back in the early 1980's. I was in Washington, D.C. at a meeting and the subject of Watergate and Richard Nixon's role came up. This fellow, whose name I cannot reveal, was Jewish, a lawyer with obvious brilliance, who wanted to leave his work as a lobbyist. He said he was really sick of the greed and intrigue, the hypocrisy and the mind numbing dead-end of his career. He had made a good deal of money, loved his wife, but feared the family environment's effect on his children. What he wanted to do was pro-bono work as an advisor on educational policy.

He asked me what I thought. I very quickly told him that I thought it was an absolutely wonderful idea, providing he seriously meant it.

His reply was that he meant it just as Josephus had meant to stop the Jewish revolt against the reign of Nero!

I was gob smacked.

I had put that out of my mind, but I was interested enough in Josephus to begin looking in the writing of Sayadaw U Pandita on the subject of concentration meditation, or more accurately, *vipassana jhana*. I was hoping to learn more about the focusing of the mind on particular objects that can be directly known without the meditation of concepts. In particular, I wanted to use that part of the mind that, though it is ranging through subjects or objects, can still remain fixed on the characteristics of something from the impermanent past. Now, in my concentration, I want to deal with the suffering of the Jews through history, through the absence of self. It is in an environment of nothingness.

To start the process I will simply go to my quarters after the evening session while the two others in our cottage are out on their walking meditation. If I'm interrupted, I will still be able to use the first part of the practice as a learning experience in something other than the meditation practices I've been involved in here at Dzogchen Beara. I mention that because there are, very obviously, many methods that can be utilized to achieve a meditative state suitable to the needs of others as practitioners.

In following the writing of Sayadaw one must keep in mind his warning that one can attain a great deal through concentration and yet still be the loser. Paramount in concentration meditation is in knowing what is missing in this practice. It cannot bring about the true understanding of truth. Because of the intensity of the concentration it lacks the general breadth and inclusion of other meditative practices. Therefore, concentration meditation must have an overview that brings in the aspects of liberating intuition, or the intuitive understanding of the mechanism of the karmic cause and effect linking mind and matter. I am not at all certain that I can reach this level, but I am determined to try.

As this is yet another experiment with the use and control of my mind in direct relationship to a particular chosen subject, i.e., Jewish suffering, I am perfectly comfortable in using just concentration without the bringing of truth to me or the subject. I am satisfied that Josephus has been judged over and over and since he is the vehicle of my knowledge in ancient Jewish times and events it is not truth I am seeking. I don't think there is a better place to start than recalling Josephus. His is at the depth of human suffering as exemplified in Jewish fate.

I am very likely using methods which were not intended to be used for my purpose. Millions of words have been written about meditation and dozens of processes have been promoted, and all for the purpose of calm abiding, peace of mind and conscience, inner tranquility, deposing of ego, uprooting kilesa or torment of the mind. All of these make a better person and all together a better life and world.

I am not doing that. I am using the procedures long established to hone the processes of concentration to discover my connections to things I know and have forgotten or things I want to know and can get to know through that power of concentration in a controlled environment. This may be considered selfish and against the unquestionable good purpose of true meditation. I have meant and mean no harm to anyone. It is my boat; my voyage and my discovery only.

I, again, will use what I have learned thus far in a meditation that is not at all in keeping with the teachings of Soygal Rinpoche here at the Centre. I will take the first parts of several means of attainment and use one along with the other. I allow the name of Josephus to be observed and labeled, but not put aside. I hold a relic from the ancient ruins of Dothan in my left hand. I take the posture as recommended by most, with lower legs inter-folded, my back straight, my right hand over my right knee, this time with my eyes closed and at first conscious of my breathing. I follow my breath as I settle my mind.

In the subconscious I implant the image of Padmasambhava in his golden robes, eyes brilliant and full of humor. I start with the chant in rhythm with the rise and fall of the abdomen.

Time as time has gone.

The new scene begins as a dry and dusty picture of the ancient land of Judea. There is the constant entanglement of the conquering Roman Legions and their allies, the Parathions of Northeastern Armenia and the Syrians with the partisan Jews in revolt against their rulers. There is the annual celebration of the Feast of the Unleavened bread and there are thousands of Jews from all over the land in Jerusalem to observe the practice and pageant. I search through the names of the dozens of leaders of the revolt and those opposed. Josephus is there amongst those who envision the end of Jerusalem and Judea if the insurrection turns to armed conflict as he knows it must under John and Simon and the gangs of ruthless bandits who have joined them for riches and power.

Josephus was born destined for the priesthood and by age of 14 was a respected authority on the intricacies of Jewish law. Unable to decide which of the sects to join, he went into the desert to live with an ascetic hermit and to meditate. At the age of 19 he returned to Jerusalem as a Pharisee, then went to Rome to plead for the release of fellow priests and won. After returning, he pleaded with the nationalist leaders not to revolt, but he failed to convince them. In the ensuing revolt against Rome he was appointed commander of the northern most-region, Galilee. There are five other regions, each with their own commander. Disappointed and disillusioned, he still opposes the war and its extremist leaders.

He is captured by the Romans, but saves himself by prophesying that the Roman commander Vespasian will become emperor, and when that actually happens he is freed. He spends the rest of the war with the Roman forces because he is under suspicion as a traitor to Jerusalem.

So favored by Vespasian and his son Titus, Josephus is given a home in Rome, citizenship, a wife and a pension. He takes the name of Flavius Vespasianus. He has three children, only one of whom survives. He divorces his wife and marries a Jewess from Crete who gives him two more sons. He is a prodigious writer, but his accounts confuse me as he rambles through these stories without chronology and often geographic location. He drones, he excuses himself, but there are no others of his stature and no others I trust. I am at his mercy in the pouring forth of the tales and the sequential order is lost in the beginning. He has an extraordinarily high opinion of himself, saying that no one else could do what he has done. He writes and speaks in an analytical fashion, but still not in the order of happenings.

In my concentrated meditation I first see Jerusalem being defended by three walls with only a single rampart. It is built on two hills, facing each other, separated by a ravine and there the terrace of houses ends. One is the Upper City called The Stronghold by King David and there is the Temple, known as the Upper Market. The second temple, The Citadel is in the Lower City. The third hill is opposite and lower than the Citadel and is cut off by another ravine. Ravines separate the Upper City and Temple and the Lower City and The Citadel is separated by yet another ravine. The ravine separating the Upper City and the Lower City and The Citadel is called the Valley of the Cheesemakers, which runs down to Siloam, the sweet and never failing spring. Outside the cities, there appear two hills and two ravines with steep cliffs making Jerusalem nearly impossible to access. There are large store towers above the outer walls.

Efforts to achieve a peaceful solution have twice failed. Herod has successfully fought the men of Antigonus' army, but Antigonus gains permission to talk to Barzapharnes, against Herod's advice, to try to re-establish peace. They reach Galilee and when they find an armed state of revolt and the plot to kidnap Herod is discovered, Herod refuses to go outside the walls of Jerusalem. Many spies are about and Herod learns of all the diabolical plans against him. He takes his family and his followers in flight for Masada, the fortified stronghold. Along the way he has to battle not only the partisans, but fellow Jews. His brother Joseph joins him and advises him to disperse his followers as Masada could not hold the 9,000. After arriving at the fortress he leaves 800 men there to protect the women and leaves for Petra in Arabia.

Jerusalem is looted and Antigonous is made king. Herod continues toward Arabia to get money from the King to help free his friend Phasael from Antigonous, not knowing that Phasael has either killed himself or has been murdered. The King shows no sympathy and Herod starts back from Egypt, arriving at Alexandria where he is met by Cleopatra who wants him to command another campaign, but instead he sails for Rome.

In terrible danger from a storm, he jettisons his cargo and lands at Rhodes where he is met by his friends, Ptolomy and Sapphinius.

Leaving Rhodes and arriving in Rome he applies to Anthony for assistance for himself and his nearest and dearest in Masada. Anthony is so moved that he makes him King of the Jews and plans to use him against Antigonous, whom he totally dislikes and considers an agitator and an enemy of Rome. The Senate approves the kingship unanimously.

Antigonous is already besieging Masada, but in defending the fortress Joseph is well supplied with food and a provident rain falls, filling their reservoirs. He sends sorties out and lures Antigonous' forces into fatal ambushes. Herod now has recruited an army of Jews from Italy and Greece and he marches through Galilee, gaining more support all along the way. His intent is to raise the siege of Masada and rescue his family. He is able to do so and then sets out to take Jerusalem. He offers amnesty to all those defending. The whole campaign becomes a mess with Jews fighting Jews, mercenaries and the Parathions. Herod takes the job of clearing out Judea and the bandits in the caves chose to kill their families and themselves rather than surrender.

Josephus shows his back to me and begins anew with the immortal tales of the conquest of Jerusalem by his mentor, Titus. I know not how Simon and John have gained control of the city nor do I have the opportunity to find out from him. He seems determined to be the center of the story, yet relents and pours out the incredibly sanguine revelation.

The defenders of Jerusalem are so determined to save the city, their temples and their people that they repulse Titus's onslaught by filling the breach in the second wall with the bodies of their dead. Titus is regrouping his armies.

The starvation within Jerusalem is such that they are taking the grain from the weakest and famine throughout the country is incredibly severe. The Romans again offer peace, but the partisans fear the great harm done to the Legions thus far will not allow Titus to fulfill his promises.

Outside the walls the spectacle of the Roman payday becomes a psychological circus. As is the custom, the troops are paraded in full view of the Jews and advance in full panoply with the horsemen leading the charge. Every foot of ground is covered with gold and silver. From the Old Wall the whole of Jerusalem watches and counts the enemy numbers as each comes forward with perfect discipline to receive his pay.

For four days the Romans follow the pageant of the payday and then Titus divides his legions to begin construction of the platforms from which they will attack both the Upper City and the Temple. Josephus is placing his own life in grave danger by walking between the defended walls and the enemy, beseeching them to abandon the city under Roman conditions that promise respect to the Temples and will allow the citizens to go to whatever part of the country they wish.

He reminds the citizens that no corner of the earth has escaped the Romans and tells them the stronger have always won over those less powerful in arms. God is now on the side of the Romans and the Romans could wait for starvation to kill all those who could now be saved only by surrender. If they were compelled to take the city by storm, all would die and there was no real safety in the third wall which could fall just as easily as the first two.

Josephus is met with howls of derision and a shower of stones from the defenders. He changes his tactics from one of appeal to save themselves to a story of the nation's past history against the Egyptians and Assyria, then the horrible seventy-year bondage. Every time the Jews had fought with weapons, they lost because it was never intended that they bear arms. They must not invoke God as their cause.

He tells the people, "What have you not paraded before your enemies. You boast of your unspeakable crime and daily vie with one another to see who can be the worst, as pride of your vices as if they were virtues." He rails at them to throw down their weapons and think not of their unfounded pride but to save their families and the city. He says that if they think he is pleading with them to save his mother and his wife, they should kill them and take his flesh and blood as a price for their salvation. He is ready to die if that would teach them the lesson of wisdom before pride.

The partisans refuse to surrender, but the common people favor leaving. To avoid the plunder by their own people, the partisans, they swallow their gold, desert to the Romans and empty their bowels to have ample provisions for their needs. Titus keeps his word, and they are able to escape the horror of the city and are not to be enslaved by the Romans. Those supporters of John and Simon cannot be moved and persist in defending their city and the temples.

Their refusal to surrender themselves or the city is epitomized by three defenders, Tepthaeus, Magassarus and an attendant of Marianne called Ceagiras the Cripple. They pick up firebrands and rush through the massed enemy and set fire to the siege engines. With the wicker covers of the battering rams ablaze they will not be driven off. The Romans are enveloped in the flames and are forced to withdraw. The Jews attack violently and then quickly withdraw within the City.

Titus becomes despondent at the setback, then he voices determination. He holds a council of war and listens to the plans offered for the conquest of Jerusalem. He decides to build a wall all the way around the city and the work is divided up between competing units. The wall will contain the city and destroy it by starvation.

Starting at the Assyrian camp and continuing around

the city, the wall stretches 4.5 miles and has 13 forts; all built in three days. Truly, an amazing accomplishment. The famine becomes more intense and affects everyone in the city. Women and children cover the rooftops, too weak to stand and the streets are filled with the bodies of the old and decrepit. People are dying while burying their family members and friends and hunger stifles their emotions. Finally it silences and encompasses the whole city. The most horrible sights are the bandits laughing as they enter the houses as tomb robbers; they being the only ones other than the wealthiest who have food. They strip the bodies of the dead, tearing or cutting off the wrappings, impaling those still alive and helpless. When the stench of the unburied and decaying bodies become too unbearable they throw the bodies from the walls into the deep ravines, filling them.

Titus views this on his rounds of his wall and throws up his hands in despair, calling out to God to recognize that this was not his way of winning the war. A putrid stream runs beneath the decomposing bodies, ending at the forts in the surrounding palisade.

No one can escape. Titus builds new platforms and Josephus again appeals to the citizens and bandits to surrender. He is struck by a stone and falls, but is rescued by the Romans before the Jews can take him.

Some who have deserted the city die from gorging after the famine. Others are killed by the Syrians and the Arab units, slitting open their bellies to get the gold they had swallowed to keep the partisans from getting it. Two thousand deserters are slaughtered in just one night. The perpetrators are too many for Titus to surround with his cavalry, and the blame falls upon the Romans though none are known to participate in the atrocity. What Caesar forbid, God condemns and the whole Jewish nation has turned every means for their escape into their destruction.

The Jewish commander of the city, John, is so vile and greedy that he melts down the gold dishes, vessels and even the flagons in the Temple that the Roman Emperor August had presented to the Jews in honor of their religion. John says haughtily that they shouldn't feel badly in doing this because those who fought for the Sanctuary are entitled to it. Even the sacred corn and oil are shared with the sacrilegious crowd, who eat the corn and smear the oil upon themselves.

Manneus, the son of Lazarus, flees to Titus and tells him that 115,880 corpses had been carried out through the gate entrusted to him. Others desert and tell of 600,000 pauper bodies that had been thrown out of the gates and thousands more bodies were put in stacks inside the great houses behind locked doors. So great is the famine that some were compelled to rake the sewers and dunghills and eat the refuse they found there. Yet the partisans show no signs of regret for their reprehensible control over the city and still refuse to surrender.

Conditions continue to worsen for the people left in the city and the work on the attack platforms continues. The Romans have used every last piece of timber within a mile or more of the city, and every bit of the once beautiful land has been destroyed. The desolation is all that remains. The Romans at last finish the platforms under constant and desperate attacks to burn and destroy them. John's forces are beginning to lose hope and their sorties are thwarted by their own uncharacteristic hesitation and fear while the mail-clad Romans repel all attacks. The Jewish forces can now do nothing but retreat, returning inside the third wall to await the battering rams that will spell doom to the exhausted defenders.

Even as the rams move forward, they fall under the frenzied attack from those within the walls at the place called Antonio. With stone, firebrands, arrows and whatever comes to hand the Jews continue to counter attack.

At night and under a roof of shields, the battering ram is at work; the din of battle deafening. At last four huge stones are loosened and taken out from the base of the gigantic foundation. John had undermined the walls in his previous efforts to get to the platforms to destroy them. At this point the tunnel John created collapses and the wall, badly damaged by the rams, falls.

The Romans are in a celebratory mood. Antonio had been taken after months of siege and morale shattering losses. Their joy is suddenly obviated by yet another wall which John's people have erected, and though hastily built, none of the Romans or their allies want to scale it for it is certain death to anyone who dares to try.

Titus gathers his best of the men and makes a rousing speech to inspire them; reminding them that it is a Roman honor in battle to die while overcoming the most difficult assignments. He gets little for his effort, but one man, a Syrian who is called Sabinus, volunteers to be the first over the wall. He is black, slender and frail, unlikely a hero as Titus has ever seen. He puts his shield in front and over his head and charges the wall with eleven others. The spears, arrows and rocks come in a flood from the guards atop the battle wall and some of the eleven are quickly swept away or killed. Sabinus somehow moves forward and routes the Jews and they, thinking more are coming, turn to run, but seeing only four are there, kill them with rocks and arrows. Sabinus has succeeded only in proving his dedication and bravery.

Two days later, at 2 a.m., four Roman soldiers catch the Jewish guards asleep and kill them, sound the trumpet for attack and push the Jews back into the Temple. The Romans pour into the city, through the tunnels John's followers have built. Finally there is no room for flight and the Jews push the Romans back toward Antonio. The Centurion, Julianus of Bethynia, charges fiercely to gain control of yet another attack but slips on the stones and is repeatedly stabbed with sword and lance. He is killed after a long and brave battle, and the Jews snatch the body as their prize.

Titus orders all of Antonio to be laid flat and bare to make the future attacks easier. Josephus again calls on John to either surrender or make battle in a place of his choosing, but to stop using the Temple as a tomb of war, desecrating it in his stubborn and foolish fight. His eloquent appeal is again met first with thoughtful silence and then derision. Josephus tells the crowd that they are only prolonging their misery by fighting to protect those heinous bandits who continue to control them and to fight the impossible battle. The partisans scornfully defy Josephus and the Romans and show no regard for their fellow Jews, only taunting the Romans.

Titus has become impatient and resumes the hostilities, even against his own will. He is to send his hand picked

1,000 under Cerealis on the attack at one hour before sun-rise. The battle rages for days with many brave men on both sides dying.

One tale comes forth to me as the most appalling. Mary of Bethezub, a rich woman had brought all her possessions from Jordan to Jerusalem and once there endured the despair of being plundered by the Jewish party chiefs who took her treasure and her food in daily raids. So inflamed by the helplessness of her fight against the famine and the bandits, she takes her little baby and cries out, "Why should I keep you alive? With the Romans there is only slavery, even if we are alive when they come, but famine is forestalling slavery and the partisans are crueler than either. Come, you must be food for me, to the partisans and avenging spirit, and to the world a tale, the only thing left to fill up the Jewish misery!"

Mary then kills her son and places him over her fire and roasts him. Mary eats one half of the child and saves the rest.

The partisans appear and demand the food they smell, threatening to kill her unless she produces the meal. She replies she has kept a fine helping for them and uncovers what remains of her son.

"The child is my own and the deed is mine too. Help yourselves. I have had my share. Don't be softer than a woman or more tender-hearted than a mother. But if you are squeamish and don't approve of my sacrifice, well, I have eaten half so you may as well leave me the rest. The partisans turn away, not in shame, but in shock.

When told of this, Titus is shaken to the core and again calls upon God to see that this was not his doing as he had offered the Jews peace, self government and amnesty for everyone. They had rejected this in favor of war, famine in place of food and they had tried to burn the Sanctuary when he was trying to save it for them.

He then vows to bury the horror of infanticide and cannibalism along with the remaining ruins of their insane country. He again attacks on August 8, but is beaten back. Titus wearies of losing so many men against an already destroyed city and orders the gates of the city set afire. At this point, even though the Jews appear to be more than just defending their city, two of the most bloodthirsty of Simon's men decide to desert him. Titus is urged to kill both Ananus and Archelaus for their cruelty to their own people, but he keeps his pledge and lets them go.

The fire set against the gates melts the silver cladding and the interior wood burns with the attached colonnades. The Jews are dumbstruck at the ring of fire surrounding them and the Sanctuary is in flames. The next day Titus orders his men to put out the fire and to set a road by the gates.

The Roman soldiers, sensing vast riches and against orders from Titus, rush forward and set the Sanctuary afire once again. Titus rushes to put out the fire but his soldiers disregard him. While the Sanctuary burns the looting continues despite Caesar's practice of killing those who disregarded his orders. On Temple Hill the flames trap those huddled there, too weak from famine and battle to do more than moan as their Sanctuary burns. The Romans are now in full blood lust, killing everyone including the poor children held by their mothers.

The terrorist hoard somehow presses the Romans back

and they continue the battle. The Romans, seeing the futility of trying to save the Temple set fire to the outer buildings and regain control of the walls. The party leaders abandon the three towers and seek refuge in the ravine below Siloam. The carnage continues into September, and the slaughter of innocents goes on.

Titus orders that only the men who fought them be killed and everyone else is to be taken alive. Men in their prime are herded into the Temple and shut into the Court of the Women. Those involved in the plot are executed by the freeman Fronto. Hundreds are to be marched in the triumphant procession and thousands sent to Egypt and hard labor. Eleven thousand die while Fronto is sorting them out. Some are sent to the provinces as entertainment in the theatres, to be killed by the sword or wild beasts. Those under 17 are sold.

The siege has killed over one million and one hundred thousand have been made prisoners.

For the second time the city has been laid to waste. John was sentenced to life in prison and Simon is to be executed after the triumphant procession. The city is destroyed and the Jews are dispersed throughout the provinces. Titus marches his centurions on the long journey back to Rome and on the way holds victory celebrations where the prisoners are used as combatants against each other. Simon is executed at the Forum.

Lucilius Bassus is now the new commander for Judea and he is to destroy the fortress at Machaerus. If he is successful the whole of the Jewish nation will be subject to complete Roman rule and its hated people will be subdued and any chance for any further revolt will be quelled.

Machaerus, the defended area, is on a rocky hill rising to a near impregnable height. Ravines surround it on every side, so deep and so overgrown that to pass through them seems impossible. The one on the west is seven miles in length, ending at the Dead Sea. Those ravines to the north and south are considerably less formidable, but are a mean logistical problem. The eastern ravine is fifty meters deep and extends to the mountain opposite Machaerus which towers threateningly over all.

The Jewish king, Alexander, has built a fort there and Herod later built walls around it and established a city. Its immense height and location overlooking Arabia made it an ideal fortress against any invaders. He also built a wall around the summit with towers 90 feet high on each corner. In its middle Herod has built a palace of incredible size and beauty with many reservoirs to catch the scarce rain water.

Bassus reconnoiters the siege routes and evaluates the possibility of a quick conquest. As with Jerusalem, his men build a platform to capture the town in the first stages. The Jews set out to test the strength of the Roman legions with the plan to surrender the town and hold the fortress above. One of the young men in the city is Eleazar, a leader in the sorties. But during a lull in the fighting he goes outside the gates and is swept up by an Egyptian soldier called Rufus and carried off to the Roman line. He is stripped and taken to be viewed by the defenders and flogged. As Bassus sees the sympathetic reaction he has a cross set up for Eleazar's crucifixion. Eleazar pleads with the defenders to save his life by surrendering. Bassus agrees and when the people in the town hear this they plan to open the gates and escape in the night. As soon as they open the gates those who had negotiated for Eleazar's life inform Bassus of their plan and only a few escape. The remaining 1,700 are massacred and the women and children sold as slaves.

Bassus now rushes to the Forest of Jardes where those who escaped from Jerusalem and Machaerus have gathered. He surrounds the area with the cavalry and orders the infantry to cut down the trees where the Jews are hiding. The Jews, with no way to escape, attack. All 3,000 are killed, including the commander, Judas, who had escaped Jerusalem by following the sewers out of the city.

Bassus becomes ill and dies. Falavius Silva is the successor and only the fortress Masada remains in the hands of the rebellious forces. Masada is a rock rising 1,200 feet above the plains between the Dead Sea and the Judean Mountains, 600 yards long and 250 yards wide.

Silva uses the captive Jews to bring water and food supplies as none are available to his men. There are only two paths on which the plateau fortress can be approached. One, the Snake, starts at the Dead Sea and the other, the less difficult one, is from the west. The Snake is a winding 3.5 mile march and on either side is a deadly abyss. At the top is a limestone wall 18 feet high and 12 feet wide with 37 towers 75 feet high. Into the rock on either side are cut huge tanks to hold water.

The western approach to the fortress is protected by a large fort. Inside are huge reserves of food, oil, wine, weapons and wrought iron and bronze as well as lead. Herod, afraid of rebellion or Cleopatra's influence on Anthony to attack, had prepared his fort and his palace with astonishingly large supplies.

With the encircling wall in place Silva builds an iron clad tower on top of his man-made stone pier 300 feet high at the point called the White Cliff, 450 feet below the level of Masada. From the tower the ram was built and with it a small breech is made in the battlement.

Inside the defenders build a second wall of wood and earth which could absorb the blows. Silva had it set afire. The defending commander asks his men to stand against the Romans to death. Some, but only some, agreed to his appeal, but too many are wavering in favor of slavery. He argues strongly to keep together and warns of what is certain to happen to their families if they are to give up their long fight. Rather than be made slaves or killed by the Romans the families are gathered together. The commander's impassioned plea is taken up and the consequence is the sight of the men killing their own families, then heaping all their treasured possessions together in the center of the fortress and setting it alight. The final act is to put themselves beside the family they had killed and those selected for the gruesome task then cut their throats, then kill each other with the final man killing himself after setting the grand palace ablaze. Nine hundred sixty two die, thinking no one is left to fall into Roman hands.

From the underground conduits that bring water into the fortress comes an old woman, one other who is related to Eleazar, and five little children who have hidden while the suicide pact was being carried out. They tell the Romans what has happened.

It all ends on the 15th of May in the year 73 AD; a horrible seven years after the first partisans had revolted to keep Jerusalem from enslavement.

THE TINY RELIC FROM DOTHAN, a mere shard from an oil jar, drops from my left hand and I return to the reality of another storm on the Atlantic below the cliffs of Dzogchen Beara. I am shaking, not from the cold wind now rising, but from the terrifying brutality and greed of those who commanded Jerusalem. I arise and find my way to my bed to warm myself and to sleep in exhaustion.

EPISODE 5:

LUFTWAFFE FLASHBACK OR TRANCE?

WHETHER OR NOT the experience last night was a flashback or another self-imposed trancelike state is immaterial. What I'm finding out about the process is an important part of the personal puzzle of attainment. I am not yet frightened, nor am I unusually apprehensive. I've lived a full life-time involving myself in rather extraordinary experiences and what I've just gone through is, if anything, only the thin edge of a wedge I intend to drive into my subconscious.

What I am about to say I have said before, but it is imperative that I make defensive statements. The auto hypnosis, if that is what it is, is not what I came to Dzogchen Beara to learn about, but if the meditative practice is pushing me further than intended by my teachers, that is my concern only, and not their responsibility.   What I am beginning to be concerned about is that I have very definitely violated their boundaries of inclusion and while using their ancient and very safe means of reaching the field in the mind where I am at peace, I have either deliberately or accidentally deviated from the norm and entered into something I neither understand nor do I particularly wish to.   I can quit the journey or I can continue and feel increasingly guilty.   It has been said that there is a bit of larceny in all of us, and I am beginning to feel that I possess an incredible amount of untapped guile as well.   There is a fine line between cunning and deceit, and I am not sure on which side I am presently standing while waiting in this near state of mendacity. For lack of a formal term, to me it is intuitive intelligence.

Even in having said that I neither understand nor particularly wish to be in this less understood arena of mental condition, I am not being entirely truthful.   The truth is I do want to be able to continue and find out where it will take me.   I am quite certain that I am still sane and relatively rational and that I can still stop the train at any place or time I want, but the point is I don't yet wish to stop.   I will continue to go to the shrine and continue to meditate in the usual way.   I am learning, slowly and probably not very certainly, that I am less interested in the meditation than I am in the myriad aspects of the lives and minds of the great teachers.   The incredibly difficult scholarship of the followers of Buddha is something that seems incomprehensible in its discipline and dedication.   That such minds existed and were capable of transcending the limitations of normal intelligence is an uncompromising challenge to me.   Some westerners seem to have managed to cope with the concept of the mind within the mind and the rest of us are left open mouthed in wonderment and intellectual intermediacy. It doesn't seem possible that these levels of revelation from the massive maze of corporate knowledge can be held in the physical mind of anyone. But it is, or at least a part of the total, and there are those among us who can make an effort at enlightenment through the instructions given by Buddha and his followers. To get there is the most difficult of processes and there are infinite waysides and stopping points where the mind can be refueled by its own energy and by that indefinable something I must call inner knowledge, for I lack a better, more comprehensive name. Pandita might simply call that labeling, then again he would have passed that by as being something everyone should know if they're following directions.

For some reason it seems to me that those most capable of coping with the circumference of such mind boggling proportions are the Jews. I cannot say with any degree of certainty that they have traditionally been the better scholars and analytical thinkers, but there you are. Is it because they have always been those left to do the heavy lifting, or is it because they have chosen the less easy tasks? I asked a friend, Dr. Frank Gold about it and he dismissed it with the statement that it appealed to the Jewish mind because it has no restrictions and it possesses the quality of creative generosity which is incumbent in their faith, if not their personal make-up. His words, not mine.

Buddhist tradition would, I suppose, label or categorize meditation practice under three clear headings. There would be mindfulness, concentration, and wisdom, or *sila*, *samadhi*, and *panna*. It is pretty clear to me that I do the middle one the better of the three. I'm better equipped, at the moment anyhow, to keep on with that as being the closest one to my purpose: the world of trance. We all function best in our primary modality and sound seems the most fitting for me to use in getting to that state.

I am setting forth for myself a task which has nothing to do with the spirituality of the true meditative purpose. I am, and I keep saying this, using the means and methods of great masters of the mind and spirit to reach a condition over which I have only the signal on my wrist watch to, hopefully, bring myself back to a state of ordinary consciousness.

As my mother's family came from Germany I have the genes of that ancient people. In my travels there I have been most attracted to the region now known as the Tyrol. I am most curious to see if there is a connection between my heritage and historical happenings there or anywhere near there. What happens when I become German and at what point am I able to enter the geographic and historical Germany or what preceded its nationalization? This would most certainly not appeal to the Jewish mind I have just mentioned, but it is the geographic location of my earliest people. What was it to be a true German?

It is a Tuesday, and between sessions and the Dzogchen Beara community is now devoid of visitors. The cottage has no other occupants and it is as silent as nature allows. I have started by playing the Tibetan Master chants, beginning with that of my master, Guru Rinpoche: Padmasambhava again. It is the Tantra and the mantra is OM AH HUM VAJRA GURU PADMA SIDDHI HUM. At first the deep, deep bass voice of the chant is creating space and vibration shifts, reminding me of a sonic prayer wheel, but I am soon lost and decidedly trance-like. There is a seeming energy void that holds a presence in my incubated state of suspense. There is, again, a darkness about me and I am unaware of the true state of materialistic ambience; a light fog of my own perturbation. It is as grey as a Berlin morning and this isn't where I thought it might start nor is it as early in history as I would have wished. There is a man, an officer in the Luftwaffe talking and he is not wholly governed by quotation marks and has adjusted himself to the present tense. Just so.

1943 HAD NOT STARTED OUT to be a good year. What was happening at Stalingrad could not be kept secret and the question on everyone's face was what had gone wrong and how it could have happened? So far, the nation was conditioned to hearing of victories. Now, it clearly tasted the bitter defeat in the making. The signs were obvious as more and more Berliners wore the black arm bands indicating the death of a family member or a loved one.

The effort to save General Paulus' 6th Army was coming too late. It seemed impossible with the Russian winter on full blast and the doubtful ability to supply him entirely from the air. I was waiting for my name to be called, knowing that it could and would happen suddenly and I would again be transferred to the Russian front. Every pilot in my squadron was nervous and added to that was the daily, or nightly, raids by the British on our airfield, located just a few kilometers from the lovely resort city of Caen.

We were enjoying the spring-like weather there, knowing that in Russia it was a frozen hell. Soon enough there was no more wondering. My name came up, but this time there would be a stop-over in Berlin. There the weather in the capital was much colder and very windy. The people were looking worried. Here the British and American bombers flew over day and night. To Berliners, they had no set pattern and attack everything in a random manner, civilian and military targets alike. It was not the best of times to be in Berlin. All of my friends had been on one of the fronts; in Africa, Russia and most of them were dead. I tried to visit relatives and when I did I got the feeling they were looking at me and wondering why I was still alive. My aunt's son, cousin Fredrich had just died and the message had said he had died for the glory of the Fatherland.

"It is to his everlasting memory that he died bravely and for the good of the cause!" said my Aunt Gretchen.

"I'm certain that he did, Aunt Gretchen. Fredrich was always a leader."

I felt guilty as I waited to get a seat on a JU 52 to Krakow. All of us were replacement pilots and the wounded soldiers coming back from the front had horrible frost bite with fingers and noses missing. I had experienced that carnage before and expected nothing less, but the civilians who were there to meet them looked on as though they had been betrayed and I could understand that. They had been betrayed, but there was no backing out of the total commitment we had been sworn to and we were the ones to put on the brave face, come what may.

When I arrived in Krakow and before flying on to my next assignment I asked for the winter flying gear from the supply officer. He just looked at me as though I had to be kidding.

"Would there be anything else you might like, sir? Perhaps you'd like a suite for the week-end at the Dorchester in London? Nothing is impossible here, sir! Just order it up and we'll be glad to oblige. Anything at all!" he said as he spun on his heel and walked out of the Supply Room.

I was lucky my high flying gear could take almost any cold for I was heading to a field within a very few kilometers of Stalingrad. A whole squadron of JU 52's was there, loaded with material to help the German troops. The weather was murderous, ice cold wind blowing through the heavily loaded aircraft. We arrived over our field amid low clouds and a single Russian fighter coming to attack. Fortunately, he missed us by a few meters and he, too, was lucky for if he had continued a short ways further he would have been hit by our rapid firing AA guns.

It was terribly cold as I cautiously looked out for another fighter attack. The icy air came through the opening like a knife. I saw several wrecks of JU 52's on the ground, one of them still smoking. How I missed France at that moment and wouldn't have minded the cursed English Spitfire attacks over Caen and the everyday raids we encountered there. Anything would have been better than this! How little I really knew of what could happen on the Russian front on this tour of duty!

I had flown over Stalingrad in 1942 when we were told it would be only a couple of weeks and the city would fall. Hitler said this was the Russian show-down and whichever way the battle went would determine the outcome of the war. The way it was shaping up now, the city would fall the wrong way. No one really believed we could relieve Stalingrad. The general opinion was that if we had any sense left we would run from Stalingrad and retreat to the West immediately. Going into a fight you can win is one thing. This was the other.

We landed on a small air strip four kilometers Southwest of Stalingrad. It looked like a JU-52 cemetery with hundreds of airplanes wrecked. The war material was spread over the entire field. The dead crew members were just laid out upon the ground and the supply activities were being conducted in the middle of a graveyard. Deathly tired faces, scared, but still they continued to try to do the impossible. I thought of the fat Reichmarshall Goering and wished he was at the field to see it. It was, after all, his fault and he didn't know what was happening here, but it was nothing like what he had promised the German people. He had been, so my father had said, spending more and more time at Karienhall and away from the war. Perhaps at that very moment he was contentedly gazing at his collection of Flemish art in front of a blazing fireplace and with a beautiful meal waiting as he sipped his wine and studied his treasures. I was snarling mad as I looked out, freezing and shaking in the open cargo door.

I had been assigned to an FW 190 Squadron. That was about the only good news. The ground was covered by knee high snow and my sleeping quarters was a dug-out four meters under the now frozen ground. Inside a red-hot gas stove burned and several blankets were hung over the opening, serving as a door. In an odd way the place was homey. It was warm and there was the smell of coffee on the brew. The cigarette smoke was thick as a fog and through it I could make out some old faces I knew. On the table was some steaming hot chocolate and some bread. I couldn't understand my feelings nor could I fathom the true situation in the company of these men.

The Orientation Officer was an old friend and he was glad to see me. I looked into his tired face, unshaven for days. I hadn't seen him since back in August, 1942, when he had been one of those who had confidently predicted that Stalingrad would fall in a matter of days. Then the Luftwaffe was attacking day and night until there was hardly even the shell of a building standing.

I stood thawing my frozen self before the stove and then turned to a bunk assigned to me and went to sleep. It had been too late in the day when I arrived for any action, but I knew that that condition was going to change fast

When I awakened I was still tired for the heavy guns had rumbled all night and we could not even take off our flying suits. We had again been told that it was possible the Russian tanks could over-run us any minute. There was no protection of any consequence against those monstrous murder machines. I was assigned my aircraft and given the briefing for the day. It was a simple task to hear it told.

The FW 190 was warmed up and my instruction was to make a low level attack on anything that moved in the northern part of the city and to attack the Russians troops on the River Volga. The weather was clear and it was my turn to take off. In six minutes I was over the river and I made a wide circle from the south. On my map I could clearly see the German positions. I was suddenly taking a shower in Russian anti-aircraft fire and I began a run at full throttle, opening up with my 30 mm cannon and destroying or disabling four batteries in one low level pass. The Russian AA crew members were running hard to take shelter. On my left was the familiar sight of the seemingly indestructible old grain elevators, still in German hands. Over the river were the endless supply caravans coming, as always, from the east. Some HE 111's were bombing the depots and I got an RT contact with them that they needed help fast.

Now there were Russian fighters at 3 o'clock. I gained altitude and then I sighted the red cowling marking of the familiar Red Guard units. It was an unpleasant *de'ja vu* and my old enemies were blindly attacking the HE 111's and paying attention only to that assignment, unaware at that point of our fast approaching presence. I could see that on my left there was an opening into them. I was so close to them I couldn't believe they didn't see me coming. I picked the YAK with the line of victory ribbons and blasted him to pieces with one burst of the 30 mm cannons. The rest of the attacking aircraft disappeared into the nearest cloud cover. That much about them hadn't changed and I was very glad for that as I was low on gas by then and had to head toward the home base, coming right down on the deck and roaring along at near ground level. The first mission that day was over as far as I could tell and it hadn't been hard at all, at least not for those of us who flew the fighters. The bomber crews who lived told a different story; a grim and ghastly story of death around them and death on the ground in incredibly high numbers as the Russian revenge began.

Before I landed to be refueled and rearmed I flew over the Russian units, heading west. T-34 and Stalin tanks, hundreds of them! What could we possibly do to stop them? Disaster was absolutely unavoidable. I landed on the last drop of fuel. The field was in chaos. The wounded were laid out on the tarmac and some canvas tents had been erected for emergency operations. The wind was blowing the blood soaked bandages all over the field, like red-tinted banners being whipped away. The dead bodies were piled up on the left. On the right, those who were still alive were being treated by the doctors who looked like hog butchers at the market, covered with blood. The deathly wounded men were lying on the ground, their yellow unshaven faces still and quiet for the most part, some moaning and their eyes showing the hopelessness they surely felt. They were resigned to their fate, knowing they had done all that they could do, having given all that they could give. For many others it was just that they were there waiting to be killed with no idea of why or even where they were. My heart ached, but I could do nothing.

I then suddenly thought of my sweetheart Rosie and again thanked God that she was not here. If ever there was an instance in history where human enemies were being ground up into useless waste, this evacuation airfield had to be the horrible example. Nothing could be worse, or so I thought. Yet, I knew too as I had known in the summer of 1942 that if Rosie was there, the last moments of some of the woundeds' lives would have been made decent. What a great pity, I thought, that understanding life only comes with inescapable death.

I would never forget those eyes of the men as I walked among them, looking for faces I might know. It was so pitiful, so inalterably pitiful. So many so near their death that they did not even moan, some clutching their rosaries and their lips moving silently, others whose haunted faces seemed to ask me for help I could not give, but forgiving faces as well, defiant that I must represent them in the honor of their dying. I had never felt this way before in my life and I had never been in such a living crypt. My air view of death was easy. You either made it through or you were blown apart, a clean spin to oblivion and the final crash on earth, a leather envelope of pulp ending with probable cremation. So be it. That was flying; this was dying in its most prolonged and aggrieved way. My stomach lost its feeling; my mind went numb with sorrow. I had found only two crewmen I had known. The rest were soldiers, some new, some old, all quietly studying their own death.

Everyone now knew our fight to save the surrounded Sixth Army was doomed. Stalingrad would fall to the Russians soon. They would have the city encircled and we must evacuate our field, but how were we to do that with ten thousand wounded lying there in the freezing cold and wind. I had to find a way to rest and get something to eat so I could function. I went to the dug-out and found it loaded with wounded staff officers. There was hardly an inch to move and on the faces of everyone there you could see their wonder at how they were ever going to escape from their hell there.

In another thirty minutes my fighter was again ready to take off to try to protect the returning supply JU 52's from the Russian fighters. Those few minutes had seemed a lifetime. The aircraft were so loaded with wounded they could hardly take off, heading into the west wind. I could see the pilots worried faces behind their Plexiglas windows. Their job was non-stop, flying only far enough to get their wounded cargo to some safety, some form of help; some medical relief. Then back again, and out again, day and night with no rest for the flying crews of the transports. They were methodically reduced by the fighters hovering overhead and the anti-aircraft batteries which pounded them as they slowly turned over the city and desperately tried to reach a safe sanctuary for the dying inside the thin shells of their planes. The cold wind was shifting and over the narrow strip of runway; the visibility had dropped to almost zero. The exhaust fumes blended with the grey of the day and the even in the freezing death of the men there was an unmistakable smell of blood, aviation petrol, diesel fuel, vomit, putrefied, gangrenous wounds and excrement. The field was ever increasingly loaded with wrecks and a JU 52 hit one of them with the left wing while flying at full speed and just becoming airborne. The doomed Junkers cart-wheeled on the ground and broke into small pieces, spilling the wounded out over the runway, killing all of them. It was a terrible fate for those so nearly rescued.

The thought came to me that this was a terrible waste of innocent life. These men didn't die as soldiers; they died in an incredible accident in a moment of mechanized history. As soldiers we all prayed for a quick death, but these men had been first wounded, then rescued and then killed on their way to home and possible recovery. It was a cruel fate and a horrible example of what could happen to any and all of us.

Then to the flight line again where I was the last to take off with seven of our FW 190's in the air already. We were to protect about ten JU-52's trying to gain altitude and flying to the west. Then we were to search for targets of opportunity. There was no shortage of those. Three of us were flying low and the sky was suddenly clearing as it sometimes did in that area. On my left my old friend was wagging his wings for attention.

On the RT came his voice, "Rosie One, on your right. Russian tanks!"

I looked and he was right. They were not supposed to be there. It was an encirclement drive and I called the ground observer, "Russian tanks running south to north in the sector west of Stalingrad, just east of Kinyow!"

A tired voice answered, "Yes, Rosie One. They just rolled through our defense line. All hell is breaking loose back there. Take all your aircraft and attack."

We turned southeast and picked up the sight of hundreds of vehicles following the tanks. They opened up with a tremendous barrage of mobile anti-aircraft fire as we came to the attack. I gave the order to Eddie, Joseph and Nowy to attack the anti-aircraft batteries while our other four hit the white-painted tanks. The tanks saw us and knew they had our attention. On the flat ground they were making a desperate run for their lives. The churning snow swirling up made the visibility very bad. I made a sharp turn and lined up and looking at the rear end of the lead tank and came at it no more than fifty feet above ground. I was thinking only one thing and that was to kill the tank. There was no thought of safety.

"Kill the tanks, Kill the tanks!" I screamed with the faces of our dying crewmen back on the ground flashing through my mind.

The lead tank was in the green of my sight and I fired the two 30 mm cannon, hitting his engine cover. A huge ball of fire exploded.

"The fools are carrying extra fuel barrels strapped to the back!" I shouted to the others. I pulled up and the AA guns had been silenced by the three others. Now we could get at them without interference. In less than ten minutes we had left fifteen of them going up in flames. We turned around and headed back to Gumrack, landing in a snow storm. By then it was getting dark fast. The dug-out was full of soldiers, but my crew chief had saved my place and I lay down, dead tired.

It was impossible to fly the next day. The Russian winter was putting on a show with a North wind blowing hard and temperature of minus 20°F. The needle-sharp snow cut into your skin but I had no reason to go out of the dug-out. Inside, in our burrow, it was warm. My breakfast was a liter of black coffee and 1/2 kilo of dark bread, and though it didn't taste like bread I ate it anyhow. I cursed the genius of German sciences that could create bread from sawdust. You ate because you were hungry; it was 3 dk Cuker, 3 dk margarine which looked like axel grease and tasted like it as well. I asked my crew chief how he had come to end up in a mess like this. Mark just smiled and said he had been out for an adventure and got on the wrong bus. Mark, because he was not an officer, could not sleep in the same bunker, but he faithfully brought me my food and anything else he could forage by his ingenuity. I had better rations as a flying officer, but that was not going to last, that was certain.

The dugouts were getting terribly over-crowded as there had to be a place for the wounded, most of who seemed to be SS. It was 3 pm and getting dark and we had been under artillery shelling all day and it would very likely go on all night. Some gasoline storage had just gone up and the sky was lighted all around. I spent a couple of hours killing some lice, sitting on my bunk in the corner, not much more than a rough set of boards with some straw and two heavy army blankets. It was a good home for the lice, but hardly what I had believed at one time that I would have in the Luftwaffe.

Some vodka bottles were going around, trying to ease the life. Every minute or two the news would come in and it was never good. The Russians had broken through Sector 4 and our soldiers coming into the bunker had just escaped death or capture, telling the true situation in the inner city of Stalingrad. There was hand to hand fighting everywhere, Germans in one part of the bunkers and the Russians in the next part. With the weather the way it was there was nothing we could do.

In a moment of sheer insanity I borrowed a heavy fur coat and caught a courier motorcycle ride to the Command bunker a short few kilometers away where General Paulus held his staff meetings. I really don't know why I did it nor did I fully understand how the dispatch driver ever got there through the shelling, the snow-blocked streets and the sniper fire. The bunker was under a pile of rubble and there were Command Staff officers all over the place; red stripes, and I was surprised at how calm they were. A friendly Colonel smiled at me and said it was good to see some Luftwaffe officers around. I thought he was being sarcastic, but he offered me a drink of warm wine. He told me he thought it was my fat boss's fault that they were still there. I thought he must be drunk, but he continued, going on about this fat boss, Goering with his wonderful flying ma-chines had gotten them into the situation they were in. He looked at me to see how I was taking the abuse, but I only smiled and said he was right, but it wasn't just Goering. He shook my hand. He clicked his heels and threw up a right arm salute. I just kept an idiotic smile on my face. I had just seen a case of the recognition and acceptance of a man's fate with absolute resolution.

Under that pile of rubble there were the German High Command Headquarters, hospitals, field kitchens, radio room, the RT and teletypes sending messages. The operators did not show any good news and General Paulus was standing in the middle of his staff officers. I could see how terribly tired he was. His uniform was crumpled; officers were coming in from the other bunkers. Many of them were wounded but still there to report to their General. A fine dust was floating in the air from the masonry which was taking a tremendous pounding from the salvos of Russian shells. You could hear the thump: one, two, three, and pause. They started shelling early in the night and I began to wonder how I could get back to my place to fly if the weather cleared.

On the surface was instant death. An SS officer was standing near me and he said I looked worried. It was a friendly face, with a black patch over his left eye. I told him I had come to hear the General and get good news, but there hadn't been any good news and now I was worried about getting back to my place. The dispatch driver who had dropped me off was nowhere around.

"I have no idea how or why I got here." I looked at him and he looked at me.

He said, "It always amazes me how flying officers seem to get lost on the ground!"

"I agree with you whole-heartedly, but that does not solve the problem."

"Let me assure you, there is no solution. Does that help?" he asked.

He was a tall, athletic-looking officer, dressed in fatigues of white snow camouflage. He asked me if I'd like to smoke and I thanked him but declined. He pulled out a liquor flask from inside his tunic.

"Obersturmfuhrer Hunczman from Berlin at your service," he said.

In a moment we were friends. We had attended schools just a few blocks apart. We had common friends, knew some of the same girls. In this small world we exchanged news.

"Remember Aki?"

"Yes."

"He's dead. So is little Aljos. So is Frank. So is Joseph. He died in Africa."

We took big gulps of the rum and I could feel the alcohol warming my body, numbing my feelings and the worry was sliding away. I could laugh. He then looked at his wrist watch.

"I tell you what, Erich. I am going on patrol with my men. Come with me and I'll deliver you to your place. OK?"

Stunned by the rum I had previously disliked, it seemed the best offer I would get. We walked through an underground labyrinth where I could clearly hear the machine guns firing. He told me not to worry, that it was almost over and that it was like that for a while every night. Then the Russians would take a rest. In a large room were about fifty

SS, all young and fearless. They looked different, without heavy worry on their faces. I looked around. The Knights Cross was hanging proudly around the necks of many of them. They were busily checking out their weapons, the Panzer Faust machine pistols. One of them was a cocky appearing fellow who said, "You're now one of us!".

I looked at him and had to agree that I guessed I was now one of them. He laughed loudly and said I just hadn't better let the Ivans catch me because they would give me a special treatment. Everyone then laughed and I had to laugh too, though I didn't think it was that funny. Still laughing they handed me an M 42 machine pistol and some hand grenades.

Three of the SS left the bunker to reconnoiter. The order was given to take their last smoke and to get ready. I look at them and I couldn't help it, I said the old Latin phrase, "Ave Ceasar Muruturiet Salutante." "Let's go men,.

"Jesus Christ! Did I just hear the Pope?" said one of them and 20 of us left the bunker!

Between the stacks and piles of bricks we emerged to the dusty, cold and pitch black night. Only the Russian shells lighted the sky, coming from the East, raking the rubble, once a city, with salvos. The word came to stay close. We climbed over heaps of bricks, tying to use the remaining walls for protection. Stopping, my friend passed the word to be quiet.

"A Russian patrol is only a few feet away," whispered his Sergeant.

We could hear them talking to each other like they were on a Sunday walk. I lay down between two large blocks of stones that had once been the entrance to a building now extinct. A Russian was walking a few meters away, dressed just as we were in white camouflage and in a minute they were past us. We waited, then followed them, 20 phantom SS, emerging from the rubble, all of us looking alike. We looked so similar to the Russians that I was near panic. We were now just a very few meters from them. The word came from the front to raise our right arm, this way we would know for sure who was an SS and who was Russian. I looked to my right and the SS there was wearing a heavy Russian fur cap. How was I to know if he was one of us, but it was a common practice to take a fur cap from a dead Russian because they were much warmer. I looked at his face and he was smiling at me. It seemed to me a very ghoulish smile in that faint and distant star-shelled light.

The moon was also giving us a slight light through the blue haze that was floating over the wreckage of the city. It was like a landscape of the surface of the moon. The shelling had stopped. I asked Hunczman what was wrong.

His grinning face was close to mine. He said, "It's midnight and time for the Ruski to go to sleep." Now, he said, "We will use only the machine guns and watch for the snipers. We'll rest a bit, but be careful not to be above the line of the bricks because Russian patrols are never farther than thirty meters away. We will follow them."

I was right beside Hunczman and I had no idea what he was planning. Was he going to ambush them? He stopped and turned, "We will follow the Russians and find out where they were going," he calmly said.

There were no more pockets of Germans here. We were in a modern-day no-man's-land that didn't differ much from those of World War I. Around were the ruins of some larger buildings and there was smoke in the air and the smell of food. Against a wall there was a Russian field kitchen, a few gas lanterns giving some light and the Russians were lying around on the ground. On two wheeled carts were loads of bread, white bread! A Russian was handing over loaves to the soldiers. We were just a few meters away and I asked Hunczman if we were going start shooting them.

In response, he calmly stood up and walked toward the cart. The Russian handed him a loaf of bread. He turned and walked into a shadow and in a few seconds he was back laying down beside me, chewing on the bread.

"Now it is your turn," he said. He told me not to be nervous, to just do as he did. I stood up, stepped out of the shadow, and walked around the barrel. The Russian didn't even look at me. He handed over the loaf, still warm, and I disappeared back into the shadow.

Hunczman simply said, "Next," and in fifteen minutes later all of us were finished with the bread. The Russians disappeared in the dark and only the kitchen crew stayed.

Hunczman then said, "Let's go. I'll take you back to the Luftwaffe bunker before dawn and all of the shit starts again."

He told me it was not a big thing; that they tried to steal Ivan's food every day. He smiled and said they had more than we did.

"It's no more dangerous," he said, "than just being in Stalingrad."

He was right.

I was sure we would ambush them, but he said there was no point in it. It was a kitchen and if we did that they'd never come back and there would be no more fresh bread.

Some of his men spoke Russian and sometimes they even got soup and sometimes a piece of meat.

"What a life, eh, Erich?" he said. I thought I could read his resignation to fate in that statement, but perhaps he really did think he could get out.

With one other SS trooper we somehow made our way back to my own command area. Hunczman just waved off and left. The SS trooper stood looking at me for a moment and then said, "Auf Weidersien."

The sky was a light lilac with the red sun coming up in the East. It occurred to me that everything including the sun was coming from the East, but it was now quiet and I was dead tired. I would be happy to fall asleep in my own bunk. I never seemed to have good luck with visits or satisfying my curiosity away from the Luftwaffe. I felt safer in the sky. I fell onto my straw pallet and when I woke up in was a day later and it was still snowing. No flying for another day, at least.

Some JU-52 was trying to land but it was a disaster. A HE 111 was just taking off, loaded with some important personnel who had been ordered out. They crashed together, killing all. People thought that General Paulus would leave the troops behind and that was bad news, but the worst news now was that the army which was supposedly trying to relieve the Sixth had been crushed in their efforts to crack the Russian rings surrounding Stalingrad. No one ever heard from them. I was trusting to my good luck to fly my plane out. It was in good condition, but it was useless in such weather. It took hours just to start the engine. When I could I would take off, flying in zero visibility to drop one 250 kilo bomb hoping it would hit something. If I was lucky there would be some black smoke coming up but I'd never know what I had hit.

The Russians were everywhere. The Sturmovich bombers were coming over every hour. Many of them crashed into the ground with full loads of bombs. Wave after wave of Russians were attacking the remaining German positions and the dead were piled on top of each other, but more and more and more bombers kept coming. Hundreds and hundreds of T-34 tanks came crashing through the snow fields and over the piles of bricks and timbers. Our intelligence service said they had been destroyed, that there were no more tanks and no more aircraft. I wished the fat pig in Berlin and his propaganda minister friend Goebbels was here. I would have gladly shoved them in front of the tanks myself. Around the Army I didn't feel very comfortable in my Luftwaffe uniform. I drew a lot of degrading remarks, but I could understand and just stayed quiet. There was now no hope for the soldiers.

I gave my extra underwear to be ripped up for bandages for the wounded. For days I slept in my flying gear, taking off only my boots and washing my hands and face. I would have given anything for a hot bath, or a cold bath, or any bath. The food rations dropped to half but I was still there, alive and unharmed. I wondered why.

The men in the dug-out changed many times. New faces every day, the old dead and wounded taken away. I tried to learn what had happened to Hunczman. Was he dead or alive? Finally the word came from one of his men that he had been unlucky on one night patrol. He was dead. His Corporeal said it wasn't really unlucky; it was just that he was dead. Unlucky would have been wounding or capture, as we all understood.

Within all of the carnage there existed a special world where my fiancé Rosie lived; or perhaps where I lived with Rosie.

It was created from the chaos and the fatigue, the murderous incoming shells, the bombs dropping on us night and day and the deafness it provided. I could understand how the people of London and Berlin could live and even flourish in the rains of death. One simply became so immune to the damaging pounding that you rejected it as being uneventful and hardly noteworthy to your existence. You, in fact, overlooked it as though it wasn't really happening and so were able to go on. The moments when I was airborne were unreal, too, and they helped add to the illusion that I wasn't really there, but in this world with my love.

There wasn't any mail coming in, of course. They tried to bring some in, but the priority pushed it aside and it probably ended up in some hangar in Eastern Europe or Poland and then became fuel for the fire to keep a mechanic temporarily warm enough to work for short bursts between the cold and exhaustion. I told myself I didn't care. It was better if I didn't hear from her. It might have been nice, I concluded, but it wasn't at all necessary because I had this fuzzy corner of my mind where I lived with Rosie and the thoughts of being with her there were dreamlike and pleasant.

I didn't get to the point where I was having full-blown conversations with her, but I did find myself smiling or saying just the words "yes" or "please, Rosie!" I would nod my head back and forth in pleasure as her face appeared before me and that soft hair I would brush from my face in my sleep as she hovered over me, teasingly, as she always did before she kissed me.

I took the small portrait of her and the one of us together, taken in her mother's garden on my last leave and put them in between two pieces of light Plexiglas. I taped them to the instrument panel so I could look at them whenever I wanted, then took them down and put them in the thigh pocket of my flying suite. When I found that uncomfortable I put them back by my bunk where they would tremble under the pounding of the bombs.

Then I found I didn't want to look at them anymore and so hid them from myself in the bottom of my rucksack. I awakened one night with a deep sense of worry about having lost them and spent several minutes swearing and tearing out my meager clothing supply to find them again. Those in the bunker who heard me and saw me didn't complain or ask what was wrong or even declare me mad. They must have known.

The final straw came when I took the pictures and slipped them into my parachute pack as I checked it. But my room for Rosie lived on in my mind and it helped. I don't know what my condition might have been if she had been the ordinary girl most of the men seemed to have or to have lost. But she was not ordinary and she was Rosie and so she helped carry me day after day and week after week.

I awoke on a blinding sunny day, the sky clear and cold. My plane was already warmed up and the Luftwaffe Ground Information said there was a large concentration of T-34's on the east side of the Volga which had to be destroyed at any price. We were to protect the HE 111's attacking them and then attack ourselves.

I went up to 3,000 meters and the city was covered with smoke. A fierce AA gun barrage came up at me and my instant reaction was to go higher. I climbed as high and fast as I could, but an explosion came on my left and I felt a sharp sting in my left leg. A splinter from a shell came through. My first thought, strangely, was not on my own safety but of my plane! I expected the worst, wondering if the engine had been hit, but no, she was alright and she climbed with full power. I was above the Volga, swinging irregularly from side to side to be less a target. Below me I could see trucks and tanks as far as the visibility permitted. The river was frozen solid and I had a bomb to drop. I must get lower. I let the bomb go and a gyser shot up from my bomb and black smoke with it. Trucks were sliding into the water while below me continued the rows of AA gun fire sending up their heavy barrage. I started a dive into them at full power, firing as soon as I was within range. I was so low they had no chance of hitting me. I made a sharp turn to the right and got out of there.

I could now check my wound. I had been lucky and I considered it nothing. I pulled out an inch of razor sharp steel. My flight boot had given some protection but it was filled with blood. The sky above Stalingrad was getting more and more dangerous for every senseless mission.

When I was back on the ground the wound was dressed. I went again to my bunker and sought the refuge of a few hours of rest. I fell asleep and stayed sleeping for the rest of the day and night, despite the noise and confusion, the movement and the ominous presence of death in that dirty little hole in the Russian soil.

When I woke up the cigarette smoke was thick and I looked at the tired faces. In the corner were dozens of wounded, moaning men with the sweet, pungent smell in the air, a smell of burns, wounds and blood. A young SS soldier was dying, in delirium, calling his mother. "Mutti, Mutti... ich libe dich, Mutti." Then he was quiet and died. The other faces showed no emotion, too tired, too pained to even blink.

My crew chief, Mark was standing above me with a big food container steaming. "I brought you some food, some beans and meat."

I don't know what I would do without Mark. He was worth his weight in gold. A master mechanic looking for adventure, he found more than his share. Still, in all this, the trading went on and anything was available with enough cigarettes. Mark seemed to have an inexhaustible supply of them when most needed.

Worse news came. Morokows was in Russian hands and supplies coming through now had dropped to nothing and the petrol was very nearly gone. I hoped that now they would transfer me, or had they forgotten me as they had done in the past? Would my end come here, dying in Stalingrad? The Field Police were coming and rounding up every able-bodied soldier, anyone who could walk. Cooks, doctors, mechanics; Luftwaffe men without a plane or duty were called. I was given the job of attacking the river barges in the Volga, another low level assignment with no room for errors.

We had lost most of our FW 190's doing just that. Forty kilometers on the river front was half frozen and we used bombs, again with some falling on the ice and sank some of the trucks but with no big damage. I came back with the machine gun attack, coming in lower yet. Both sides of the river were loaded with AA guns. I could see the Russian soldiers rushing to the ice to get the dead and stunned fish which the bombs had brought to the surface. I left the devils alone. My job was to strafe the trucks. I didn't waste my ammunition on the "fishermen." Full speed and as low as I could get was the only way I could avoid the AA fire and it was a miracle I hadn't been hit.

I knew what would happen if I lost my plane. I would share the miserable end of my life as a prisoner in Siberia or die of wounds if I wasn't killed outright. There were no replacements and there were no planes left to fly out. This was the soldier's life and the life I had volunteered for so I had no real legal complaint. I would worry only when the worst happened and it hadn't happened yet. The others said my life was charmed and I had to agree.

Since Morokows had fallen there were no spare parts and my engine was leaking oil. No one knew how long this could last and the possibility of a terrible end was coming fast. The Russians were breaking up all German resistance and it was a horrible sight to see what was happening here. There were wounded everywhere – no medicine, no bandages, no food. Foraging parties risked their lives to find a dead horse. The German discipline held and there were few complaints. These were the real heroes, the best soldiers the world had ever seen.

The Russians were sacrificing thousands and thousands of soldiers, attack after attack, no matter what the human cost. I was told about another meeting, the last one General Paulus held. He said this was the end, but that Hitler had forbid any capitulation. We were to fight to the finish and that meant all of us. All women personnel and female nurses were to be evacuated.

I saw Mark's happy face, smiling as usual, but with a special look.

"Sir, you are to fly out. You have orders!"

"When, Mark?" I asked, incredulously.

"Now, sir. I will service the plane."

"But, what about orders for you, Mark?"

"I don't know, sir. They said for you to leave, nothing about me."

"Then get rid of anything in the cockpit that will come out. We will somehow stuff you and Fritz in with me and the three of us will go out together."

I said a quick and soldierly goodbye to my friends, knowing that I'd never see them again.

The cockpit was not really meant to hold two, and nearly impossible to take three aboard, but when you must you must and we somehow made the room. One could thank God it was a FW 190 and not my usual ME 109! The big BMW engine, despite the oil leak, made the trip effortlessly as we took off in a blizzard and headed west. The landscape of Stalingrad disappeared down below, but never from my mind.

Our destination was yet another airfield in the frozen wasteland of Mother Russia, with yet another chance to be killed.

EPISODE 6:

INSIDE STALINGRAD

T HERE IS SO MUCH TO LEARN and so little I understand. Am I suffering from concentration exhaustion and reaching the post-meditation state where one is distracted from the equanimity and questions surface regarding these appearances as illusions or dreams?

I think I am able to stay with the object of observation, that is to say, Erich, and I am able to remain there. I am not, however, in following continuous concentration, advancing in the Vipassana practice of developing wisdom. I am, quite simply put, stuck in concentration on the one subject of this Luftwaffe pilot in World War II.

I am of World War II vintage myself and had I been in the European Theater, I would undoubtedly be deterred by hatred. I don't have that. In fact, having been in the Pacific Theater, if this figure was to have been a Japanese pilot, I might not be receptive at all because of that probable in-bred, inherent but unintended hatred; a hangover of a conditioned mental state.

Yet I don't feel I am pursuing Erich. He is there in a specific station in my mind which is now quite easily assessable. If this were intuitive, it would be a series of "aha" moments. It is not that at all. I am on a positive sequential cognitive wave of the past.

The visualization, if what I'm doing, is a niche of that. It isn't cultivating mindfulness, spiritual empowerment, or the freeing of the mind of errors of thought, so there is nothing buddhaistically good about it. I'm at a plateau of hypnotic mindfulness of my own experience within myself, and that's it. Nothing even remotely spiritual exists in what I am achieving and it is psychologically bothersome. I must accept that and continue or give it up and I won't give it up. It may be that this is experience is a part of the selfish nature of man and it may be that my ability to concentrate to this degree is making me more selfish. This is directly opposed to one of the goals I had in coming here: to become less attached to everything.

I do not believe in the pseudo-mystics who perform as media for the dead to speak through, though even in Buddhist writings they tell of previous lives or envision teachings as being revealed to them. To my imperfect way of logical thinking, the two are related in some remote degree. Erich is by no means speaking through me. He is just there, as I've said before, telling his stories and there certainly exists the possibility that anyone else can look him up if they are inclined to do so. Yesterday I thought I had said goodbye to him.

And now, I am more than objectively curious, and I return to him in his current predicament.

The Wing Commander was still at my base when I finally returned. Half the squadron had been sent to East Prussia where all hell had broken loose with the Russian Army of the North rampaging along a 150 kilometer front.

No one at the headquarters could believe it was me. Not that I had changed that much, barring my thinness; it was just that I could not possibly have survived. It was hard to believe myself and if I had been hearing my stories instead of telling them, I probably couldn't have found any reason to believe I was really back there after all I had been through as a prisoner at Ercsi and on my erratic, uncontrollable journey homeward.

I was given leave for a few days and chose to remain close by. I needed rest more than any recreation and though the rations were poor they were a great deal better than I had had during my time with the labor battalion or would likely find anywhere I might go outside the Luftwaffe. I was not denied any local pleasures; it was just that I was tired and chose to stay. I spent the most of one of those days trying to reach Rosie, having futile efforts at patching in through the hodge-podge of telephone communications. I had thought, wrongly, that if I could at least reach Augsburg or Berlin there would be some family member to whom I could give my message of love. So much for that kind of idealistic thinking. I got nowhere and settled for a letter in which I told her I had been out of action and apologized for not having written. I didn't want to worry her any further with what had been an experience I'd just as soon forget anyhow. I missed her very much and wanted desperately to see her but had another visitor instead.

The Commander himself came to me on the third day and said he needed me to fly a mission. It was to be just a quick one.

He could have ordered me to fly, as he could anyone else he had available and if he wanted to send me he could and would, without asking me. He was good enough to give me an explanation.

"The town of Tattersall to our Northwest is being surrounded by the Russians. General Klueter, the SS Panzer Division leader was in command there until he was wounded. They have all been badly hit by the anti-tank specialist and the General was himself severely wounded. Now, our information is that the tanks are to stay but General Klueter is to be evacuated. The Panzers can blow their way out but we must get him out immediately. Do you see what I'm getting at?"

"Yes. You want me to fly in there and get the General."

"Exactly! I want you to go to the Panzer Headquarters. They will give you a Fieseler-Storch and you will fly into the stadium where the unit is positioned and bring him out. It has to be done right away."

"Then I had better get started," I said.

"Yes, you had better get started. When you get back this evening we will talk about a leave for you. It would be much better than trying to telephone your family and girlfriend!"

The logic of Wing Commander Fischer was inspirational. However, something in the back of my mind clicked into place and for some reason I said, "I think not."

By the time I had said it, the Commander was already out the door.

At the Panzer Headquarters there was precision in what could have been chaos. The small air and reconnaissance detachment was the centre of activity to evacuate General Klueter. Here was efficiency and aggressive leadership. Here an officer's life was a matter of duty and from what I had recently seen at close hand, the Soviet claim to egalitarian camaraderie had been replaced by their taking extremely good care of themselves in matters of their own personal preservation.

I was driven to the command post in a Mercedes staff car and taken inside. I was in my flight uniform, ready to go, and I was assigned an aircraft without question. I was given a briefing, a map of the area around my stadium objective and told that the general was in strong concrete rooms beneath it. This then, was Tattersall.

The plan was workable. In tightening its perimeter, the Panzers had a good field of fire and excellent protection provided by the sturdy walls of the structure. From inside the tanks could fire effectively, even while the Russian mortars pounded on the concrete itself. Eventually the heavy guns would bring it down, but for now it was a good place to be.

I sat beside a little portable table in the CP and listened to the air liaison officer describe the conditions of the siege, the wind direction and velocity, my gas load and the characteristics of the enemy fire. At the same time I looked at the map and made mental notes about my probable approach, ground time and return flight. The more I looked at the map, the more bitter my recent memory.

The radio messages from the Tattersall confirmed that the general must be removed immediately. He needed whole blood and evacuation surgery which his doctor there could not perform. He was bleeding badly from a belly wound and a severe head injury, all from shrapnel. The general was respected for his disregard and disdain for small arms fire. He had reportedly said that the trouble with mortars was that you were dead before you heard them. The news sounded as though he was in desperate straights.

"I'm going now," I said. Where is my plane?"

In the distance the low rumble of the battle could be heard across the flatlands and low hills, across the sullen valleys with their dark shadows.

"The strip is just to the West," answered the liaison officer. "We have a very good Storch for you. Will you need a hand gun?"

"No, I have my own."

I was escorted by the officer and a corporal to the plane. The crew chief shut down the engine after checking it. It coughed briefly, the prop reversed twice and stopped.

I slid the map into my thigh pocket, checked the struts and landing gear, pulled the clip from the stabilizer and pressed the gas tank indicators, walked around and got in. The Storch fired up immediately, the mags checked and I re-set the altimeter. I tapped a gloved hand to my helmet, looked both ways and when the chocks were pulled, blasted the tail off the hardstand with a burst and turned downwind.

Rapidly taxiing to the end of the runway I checked the operations light signal, rechecked the magnetos and cranked it up full bore. It was, I knew, a hell of a good little aircraft and one I could have enjoyed more if the trip wasn't in the orders.

"Well," I thought, "Let's get this over with!" I popped off the runway after a hundred meters and did a climbing turn over the field. I dipped a wing to the CP I'd just left and headed straight down the road at a very low altitude. I planned to follow it straight into the town.

Even down that low I could see the smoke and dust from the Russian supply horses and wagons, cars and trucks as they forced the struggling refugees from the roads. It was a menagerie, a mixture of every conceivable kind of vehicle now being used by both sides. The Soviets must have had every horse in the area in use, every cart, every confiscated or foraged wagon.

A few artillery pieces and combat soldiers were in sight. Most of the mass was made up of conscripted labor troops. When I got above them they stretched out at least ten kilometers to the east. Even in the fields alongside the road, they pressed forward like a colony of ants returning to the stadium and racetrack.

"This is the backdoor," I thought, and was glad it was. "All I have to do is find the racecourse, land, pick up the general and get out of there." I leisurely picked out the map, checked it by finding the road I was still on and following and flew down it like a tunnel to the Tattersall.

The ruined buildings were more numerous now and I zeroed in on the city first and then my rescue area. I could see the mortars walking, three after three, into their target zones.

There it was! Now I could hear the "crack-zap!" of the

tank guns in the stadium, firing at point blank range at the buildings nearby. The buildings came down in heaps of spiraling dust as the order of marching fire meant their end. Obviously the major thrust of the Russian attack would be from the east and the tankers were now clearing the area, ready to go roaring out of their lair and to blow the enemy out of their way as they made their escape.

I could feel the hundreds of concussions as I bored into the smoke and dust. I made the approach without circling, creased the open end of the horseshoe-shaped complex and streaked into the bowl. The fixed high-wing and the fixed landing gear meant I must fly the Storch into the ground, then throttle back, dump the flaps and start braking immediately.

As I did that I could also see the explosions in the stands and at the far edge of the track's infield and remaining grass and hedges.

I cursed. "They'll be walking them right in here next!"

Then I saw the signal from a large gate and underground walkway entrance. Pulling up close enough to make the stretcher bearer's job easier, I left the engine running after I parked in a spot with room to pull the general, the Storch and myself out in a hurry without having to turn around once he was aboard. As I jumped out to dash to the entrance and shelter I looked for shell and mortar holes to avoid in take-off. There were none so dangerous that they couldn't be negotiated. I felt both luck and apprehension as I ran toward the hole in the concrete.

"In here! The general is in here!"

"Then let's bring him out!" I yelled. "They'll be shelling us harder now."

I made it to the shelter as the "kawoomping" of the Russian mortars increased and their main target was now becoming just the stadium. Whether or not they knew what the plane was there for was moot. They were taking no chances and the tempo of fire increased by the minute. "Do you have room for the general's doctor and his nurse?" asked an SS Panzer officer.

"Yes, I can take them if they're ready," I said, walking to the throat of the tunnel. "Don't you need them here, though?"

"Not really, Captain. We can handle our own with the corpsmen we have."

Just then General Klueter was brought out on a rigged stretcher and gurney. His head was bandaged, and the white sheets and blankets over him were showing blood. "Oh, I thought, what the hell!" I was familiar with the signs of death and though the General was sedated, his face was ashgrey, slack and dead-skinned.

The mortars continued to crash into the stands, the infield and the track. I looked back toward the raised entryway and walked with the general, the doctor and the nurse, the corpsman and the adjutant toward the light.

There was a flash of fire and the simultaneous sound of a mortar shell as it blew up the Storch.

The doctor stood staring and dropped the wrist of the general, then reached down alongside the cart to pick it up and put the hand and arm under the blanket.

"General Klueter is dead. It doesn't matter," he said.

"It doesn't matter? What the hell are you talking about, it doesn't matter?" I said. To myself I said, "I just got out of this filth three days ago! I don't need any more of this!.

There I was, back to where I had started from four and a half weeks ago when I'd been blown out of the sky and into the Hungarian geography by some ignorant peasant who had been taught how to shoot! The difference this time was that there were no partisan civilians to take me away. I was amongst the most hated of the Russian enemies: the SS Panzer troops. I was the lone air officer. If the Soviets didn't kill all of us with the damnable mortars I was sure they would do it with small arms fire, no matter how the dead General had personally chosen to ignore them.

All I could think of at the moment was how bad my luck had become as I cursed my fate. This time, there was no chance.

"Call the Panzer Headquarters and ask for a relief plane!" I yelled.

"There's no point to that. We are to stay here. It was the General who was to be evacuated, not us."

"Then call my headquarters for a plane for me!"

"Yes, Captain."

The call was transferred into the squadron from the SS.

"I want to talk to the wing commander!" I said.

"He's right here."

"Let me speak to him!"

"Yes, Captain," came the commander's voice. "What is the situation?"

"Colonel Fischer, the General is dead. He could not have survived. The Storch was destroyed by mortars. Can you send another plane in for the medics and me?"

"Are you making a joke, Captain? We have no plane to spare and the medics there will find something to do!" He switched off before I could ask him about what I was supposed to do. His answer had been clear enough.

I knew I was going to die if I was taken this time. Beyond a doubt, the black-uniformed SS Panzer men would be shot where they stood… not to mention what was ahead for the poor nurse.

The second in command to the general was a Major Heilman. He only shrugged and said, "What can we do? It looks like you're one of us now!"

"What can we do? You want to sit here and wait for the Russians to come and take you to lunch? Weren't you supposed to break out and shoot them up?"

"Yes, we were. Things have probably changed. We've heard nothing for two hours and we really don't know the terrain to the west. We came here from the north. Our last observer was to our east and we had no one in any other direction."

"Then don't wait for new orders!" I reached into my right knee pocket and pulled out the map. "Do you know where you are and how to get out? Look right here, Major Heilman. You can easily do it. It's virtually an open road where I came in. It's only being used for supplies. There isn't even a mortar unit set up out there!"

"You're sure?"

"Major, I flew in here using that road like I owned it just twenty minutes ago. I'm absolutely sure it's a good way out. We can crank up the tanks and go, just like that!" I said with all the enthusiasm I was beginning to feel.

"I've got more tanks than I've got drivers," he grimaced.

"So you leave some!"

"They're like new. Hell, most of them are new!"

"Perfect!" I said. I'll drive the lead tank!"

"You'll what?" he asked incredulously.

"Drive one out!"

"I have a lot of tanks, but they aren't built for beginners and one beginner can screw up the whole run for everyone else!"

"I can drive a tank as well as anyone. I'm no amateur."

"You can drive a tank? An airplane, yes. A tank, I don't think so!"

The truth of the matter was that I had fairly good training and information from the better days when tanks of the army surrounded the aerodromes to keep the Russians off our tails when the raiding parties were sent in to blow up the Stukas that Rudel had all over the place. I'd pretty well learned their operation during the off-duty times and before that I had received training in the tanks and with the engineers at the military school.

"I'd better lead then," I said. "I have the map and I have just been over the terrain so I know where we are and where we should be going. The tank is the best way to get there."

Major Heilman called roll. He had 15 drivers, himself and me.

In a matter of just a few minutes the new tanks were fueled and running. The others were ordered destroyed immediately below the stadium. They were not to be burned. They poured sand in the fuel tanks and then put some plastic explosives to work. It was like doing business with professionals and there was no confusion here. The tankers knew they were not running away. They were going to get their chance to fight again.

The crews then manned their assigned tanks and the service personnel prepared to strap and tie themselves to the outside of the turrets. All guns were reversed and locked in trail with the three meters of the gun stuck out the back.

The Tattersall was blocked by a huge ornamental iron gate weighting more than half hundred tons and welded shut. It was locked and barricaded. Quickly the barricades came down, but there was still the gate to contend with and no time to cut it open. That would have signalled our intention of coming out.

My Panther tank weighed about 25,000 kilos and it had two 12 cylinder aircraft engines, each generating 900 horsepower. The lead tank, me, must knock the gates down and if I didn't I'd be over-run and bulled over by the other tanks on their way out. I would be just as dead then as waiting for the Russians.

Major Heilman said, "Don't hesitate, Erich. Go like hell! It will go through!"

My observer at the hatch said the men were ready. I tapped his booted foot to indicate I was ready, too. He closed the hatched and I revved up the engines, released the braking set and the tanked popped its nose high in the air, settled and lunged ahead.

We hit the gate and it was blown wide open!

For hundreds of years the huge cobblestones around the Tattersall had laid there, never having been disturbed by the burden of traffic. Suddenly these huge stones were torn loose and thrown 15 to 20 meters into the air, spraying like a sprinkler hose as the tank treads heaved them in every direction.

The tank group was now running at 50 to 60 kilometers per hour and to hell with the treads. They only had to last less than 40 kilometers and my only thought was to find the right road and get on it.

There was an ochre-colored house at the corner that marked the route to the southwestern road leading out of the city. I jabbed the right brake a little too hard at the turning and with the tanks nose in the air and the weight of the gun in back, we tore the side of the house completely off. The rest of it then collapsed.

Now on the road, the radios behind me kept yelling like a cheering section with a new game hero. "Faster! Faster! We're coming up your back! Look out! Here we come!"

On both sides of the road were the centuries-old mulberry trees. In the prism mirrors I could see the trees on the right being snapped off. The tanker running in the ditch was knocking them off as easily as if they were sunflower stalks. Half a meter or more around, cracked off completely just as though they weren't there. Horse carriages and cars which had been abandoned or pushed into the ditches were crushed flat.

In front, through the slit, I saw soldiers, trucks and horses, supply wagons, all running toward us, not realizing it was enemy tanks coming at them. That mass of humanity, soldiers and the supply vehicles were crushed as the tanks met them. The supply column was six kilometers long now, and the tank treads slipped and ran on them and not the road any longer.

I saw them in front of us, the faces as they hit the periscope. It was like running full force and mad through the gutting room of a huge slaughter house.

Those of the service people who'd tied themselves onto the lee side of the turret saw very little. They were taking a terrific beating from the trip but they were high enough above the mass and most would survive.

A little car, Italian I think, came right at our faces as my tank swallowed everything before it in speeding gulps of humans and horses and all else in its way. The car was devoured as though it had run into the maw of a huge mechanical monster.

After that the ring was completely broken and we turned to the northwest again and after 20 minutes of slower running, braked to a stop.

All 17 tanks had made it!

But, what a sight we saw as we opened the top turrets and climbed out for air! What confronted us was the grisly result of the flying wedge of Panther tanks through the Russians, their animals and their supplies.

It was the most gruesome thing I had ever seen. There were heads, hands, fingers, arms, legs, torsos, mud, horse slime and hides, blankets and even something that looked like bread hanging and dripping from the treads. Body parts hung from every corner, every hook, angle and protrusion!

At the gun turrets our tanks service crew members stirred slowly like zombies from their stupor and lifted themselves as best they could and with help from the others as they tested their broken limbs in slow motion. They helped each other undo the straps that held them close to the stench from the engine-burned flesh and hair. Some, it turned out, had been killed by the torn up cobblestones and other objects we had crashed through in our wild and terrible dash.

All the tanks were drenched in blood and the running gear was like a giant grinder, having been fed by the nearly meter-wide treads that tore at everything they could reach and grip. Now the Panzer unit had to re-group and organize their next move. It would be without me!

"How will you get to your Staffel now, Captain?" asked Major Heilman.

"How do you think I'm going to get there?" I patted the steel armor with my hand. "This is my tank!"

"I'll need that tank, Erich."

"Not as much as I do!

"Hmmn! Not as much as you do?" he asked and then, "So we took a casualty for now. I have to attend to these men and get ready to go back to work. Drop it off with your doctor and nurse passengers at the Panzer headquarters. I'll call you in. You must be about ten kilometers from there."

"About that far according to the map." I said.

"Aufweidersehn, then, Erich."

"Aufweidersehn."

"'Some life we lead,' I thought, "In with a Storch and out with a Panther! Not too many Luftwaffe pilots touring Hungary in a tank this time of year!"

After I had dropped off the doctor, the nurse and the tank I found a staff vehicle waiting for me. The Panzer's call had gone through.

As I reported in to the wing commander I recalled to him that my horrific run had been started by his refusal to send a second plane in.

He said, "Think of all the people that came out because

I didn't send a plane for you."

"True, Colonel.   That's probably very true."   Then I looked at him again.

"Commander Fischer," I said, "if you have any more assignments like that for me I want a chance to transfer to the west immediately!"

"I shouldn't wonder, Erich," he said, "I shouldn't wonder at all!"

THERE WAS A KNOCK at the door of my suite in Cottage #3. To say the least, it startled me back to the reality of where I was.

"Yes, come in," I said.

It was one of the girls from the kitchen. She looked very concerned and said very softly, "We haven't seen you since yesterday. Your little red car is still in our parking lot, but you haven't been to the shrine or taken any meals with us. We were becoming a bit worried. Are you alright?"

"Yes, I'm just fine, thank you for coming to check on me. I've, been... I've been meditating for a bit."

"You must be hungry. Why not come with me and I'll fix you something."

"I'm starved," I said, and I knew Erich was lost to me forever. I didn't want to think about him, but I wondered if he lived through the rest of the war. I doubted it very much, but one could never tell about such men.

EPISODE 7:

RECURRING DREAMS CANCELED

M Y ENCOUNTERS WITH ERICH are apparently over, at least for the moment and to some extent I am relieved. It has been a drain both physically and emotionally and I have no wish to return to the vivid experiences of his life and probable death. I've had my share of war time problems and it's time to try to get past them. The time I spent with him was worthwhile, but hopefully that series of episodes is over and I can get on with my practice and my learning here at the Centre. I cannot say with any degree of certainty that he won't come back, but I'm hoping he is safely salted away. Life and death go on.

My first experiences here were predicated on the acknowledged fact that I needed help in dealing with the death of my wife. I had attended a three day session on death and dying with a former student and friend who was well advanced in his readings, study and practice. He had insisted that we attend and learn.

Prior to arriving at the Centre I had done some reading on the subject myself and I was, quite honestly, bewildered by the complex concepts presented by the very meaning of dying and death as it relates to Buddhist near tautology. It was mind boggling in the reach and scope.

As it does not involve what we think and believe about a Christain God from our earliest childhood, it was just too matter of fact and I couldn't get a grasp of its possibilities. In their approach life and death is apparently seen as being a whole and death begins a new life. Fine, so this was a proposal not unsimilar to everlasting life; only it isn't. There are, instead, transitional realities called "bardos" and this term is used to identify the intermediate states between life and death. They present unlimited opportunities to know your innermost mind. You are there, on the very edge of what you have known and are about to be a part of what your life practices have determined for you. To repeat myself, you are what you will be. So, you have the natural bardo of your life, the bardo of perhaps a painful death (Repent, ye!), the luminous bardo of dharma or essence of things as they are, and the bardo of becoming.

The first, the natural bardo of this life is just that: birth to death and compared to all else, we all know how short life is. The death spans the time when we begin dying and when we stop breathing and at the culmination there is what is called "Ground Luminosity", or the dawning of nature. The luminous bardo is the extinguished living light replaced by "Clear Light" which manifests as sound, color and light. The last, or karmic bardo of becoming, is that time between the old life and the new. I must add that the luminosity is the good you; always there.

It's not at all as simple as I've made it sound, but in my explaining it to myself I can at least cope. There is a part of it that I do understand quite clearly and that is that through meditation one can enter different levels of consciousness. The bardo states and levels of consciousness are related to the cycle of life and death. As life takes place we experience these bardos in a variety of ways and in infinite degrees of that consciousness.

It is said that going to sleep is similar to the bardo of dying, that dreaming is likened to the bardo of becoming where you assume a state of clairvoyance and out of body likeness. The third one is far too subtle for me to recognize and that's the one on luminosity. I presume it to mean the unaccountable moments of understanding or inspiration and maybe that's part of what I've been experiencing.

I have until now, an unconfessed history of persistent dreams. I'm sure most do. One has to do with something that may have actually happened and it involves the death of a young boy. It is definitely not from my present life. I will likely never know from whence it came. The other persistent dream has to do with a little neighbor girl in my early childhood. Again, I must tell you that it is not from this existence. What I now plan to do is to reproduce these dreams on demand by, or rather through, autoscopic recollection.

Bear with me.

THERE IS A FIVE-YEAR-OLD, a sun tanned, dark, handsome

boy with an already athletic build which belies his love of summer sport and swimming. He is standing on a dock at the lakefront of his home. His given name is Ward and with him is his little brother, age two, bubbling, babbling as he watches his older brother breaking pieces of bread and throwing them into the water, feeding the fish.

"Would you like to feed the fish, too, Robert? I'll hold you and you throw the bread to them. Okay?"

Robert nods enthusiastically. He takes a piece of the bread and Ward holds him by the straps of his little blue overalls. He lets Robert stand near the edge as he clumsily casts the bread upon the water. Ward and Robert enthusiastically swing back and forth along the end of the dock. The tempo and the radius of the arc increases as Ward swings Robert back and forth, back and forth, firmly secured by his hand. It is all he can do to hold him and he quickly drops the bread and grabs the straps with both hands.

Robert looks over his shoulder and laughs as his momentum carries him closer and closer to the dock's end. Ward's face turns grim as he swings Robert hard and let's loose.

Robert swings in slow motion off the dock and as he falls his head strikes the corner of the live box, opening a gash above his left eye. He is stunned as he splashes into the water and sinks, face up, eyes and mouth open. The blood darkens over him.

Ward slowly wipes his hands up and down on the front of his T-shirt, turns from looking down and runs to the house, calling to his mother.

Thirty years later, asleep in his own room he enters a paratactic state. His eye muscles move, almost jerking as they flicker, opening and shutting again. His breathing is very shallow and fast, a whimpering breath of childhood. There is a revealing mood about him, a mask, a persona. He is dreaming in two different spheres, both disassociated with his body.

The dream starts in the fog of a marsh where he has never been. It is an immense area with magnificent cypress trees covered with Spanish moss and limbs hanging dead. He is wading in the water, slipping and tripping over slimy roots that cover the bottom. He is retching at the stench of death, though in his semi-lucid state he knows he is safe in the presence of the rotten putrefaction and the decay. He moves forward and steadies himself against the vines whose eyes watch him as they clutch at his touch. There is no sound from the creatures that surround and move forward with him. The sound he does become aware of is that of rattling breathing as though some vast and unseen human-oid is taking its last irregular and pitiful gasps. It weakens and then becomes stronger, struggling against its own fail-ing. He stops his slogging and haltingly gazes round him. A tiny ball of light bounces excitedly on the surface of the corruption and disappears beneath it. It appears again, and Ward takes hope and watches it slyly, not letting on his interest, but then moves toward it as if meaning to capture it. It moves and his feet suck up from the quick bottom and he moves, struggling to follow the ball. It disappears and reappears from beneath the surface, behind the trees, all but obscured, projecting its light and creating moving shadows as if to tease. Ward then sees, through a murky haze, in the smoke and fog, a clean white wooden dock with two people and a little boy.

At first they pay no attention to Ward and are smiling and laughing at the little boy. They then see Ward as he pushes the moss aside from the overhanging branches. The woman picks up the boy and kisses his face, his eyes, with her hideous blood colored mouth and croons. The man takes the boy and holds him tightly, kissing him, ruffling is blonde hair. The kisses turn to bites and the blood comes from the torn skin above the left eye as the man tears at him. They then throw the little boy at Ward and he is covered with the blood.

It is Robert. He tries to pass Robert back to his step-father and his mother and they again hurl the boy at Ward. Ward rescues the boy from the feces and rotting morass and puts him back on the dock. His step father laughs and whistles for Ward like a trained animal. The little boy's body sinks and Ward climbs dumbly onto the dock. The couple laugh at him. They are now naked and copulating on the dock as Ward buries his head in his arms and cries.

At this point the dream vanishes, but the sequence does continue to the mysterious, wholly unknown neighbor girl I never met.

Jana, age eight, blonde, blue-eyed, precocious, is alone in the meadow near our home, lying on her tummy on the delicate, soft moss bordering a small creek which plops its way to the Elk River. Her mongrel dog, a spotted black and white male pup, is lying contentedly by her. It is afternoon on a hot August day, with the soft breeze blowing the tall meadow grass in cloud like waves. As Jana gazes into the tiny eddy created by the rocks in the creek, a water spider skitters back and forth across the top, making only the most minute disturbance on the placid surface. A face begins to slowly form, coming from the bottom to the top. Jana lazily turns on her back, her eyes shaded by the shadow of a large red oak tree.

Grandmother is here.

She slowly drifts into her dream, seeing herself in the same meadow, squatting in a copse of willow. Distant thunder is heard, signaling the beginning of a summer storm. It is getting darker behind the silent blaze of lightening. There is no noise, no thunder, only the disconsolate sound of Jana's crying. The meadow is getting larger and the edges fade. She can no longer see the way home.

Her dog has disappeared. Slowly, silently, forms of men begin to come from each side of the woods surrounding the meadow. They are blue black with hair in bright cloth, tied into knots. Their fantastic teeth gleam like ivory in the lightening flashes that crash against the points of the spears they carry. Their bodies are naked above the grass as they swiftly and noiselessly move in time with the storm's irradiated glow. Jana then sees herself huddled helplessly in her tiny thicket, bewildered by what she feels, unable to see outside the meager walls of her protection. She crosses herself as in the great shinning light she stands now in a rainy circle of men whose smiles are animal like snarls and in whose hands the spears have been replaced by erect phallic symbols.

There is no escape other than to faint.

She then finds herself bounding through the same meadow of tall grass as she approaches her home nearby. This time, her dog disappears back into the woodland. She stops running at the gate to her backyard and she walks to the side of the house where there is a water spigot. Above the spigot is a screened open window of her foster parent's bedroom. As she bends over the tap, she hears a sound new to her. It is one of animal like delight. It pleases her and she stands to look through the screen from where the sound has come.

The first thing she sees is black cotton socks, then the monster phallus, her foster mother's bare bottom surging back and forth over it as she straddles Jana's foster father and emits snarls of joy.

"Oh! No! What is......?"

Jana's foster mother, short, heavy, and her foster father hear her and respond with surprise and curses.

"You little bitch, sneaking up on us! You get yourself in here, right now!"

Now there is total darkness.

Jana is asleep and dreaming. She returns to her meadow scene and has again reached the tap at the side of the house and the screen window through which she hears and then sees her foster mother and father making violent love in the summer's heat.

Jana has entered the house at her parent's angry command and stands, terrified in the entrance hallway. Her foster mother comes after her, eyes blazing, barefoot, bare breasted, hair flying in a rage, the front of her black kimono open and screaming at her.

Jana feels her tearing at her arm and the cotton sleeve of her pathetic little sun dress as she is pulled into the bedroom, peeing on the hall carpet in her terror. Her parents' commands and threats are no longer words as she is thrown onto the bed. There is a terrifying frenzy; a circus of physical activity. Her foster father moves around her, black socks and black mustache. She sees his penis, swollen erect and she closes her eyes tight, clenching her fists across her groin. Her foster mother pins her arms over her head with her knees and Jana opens her eyes to see her foster father's eyes, glazed and huge above her as his hands go to her crossed knees and forces them wide apart, throwing himself upon her.

Her foster mother is feasting on the miserable figure of her daughter, watching steamy eyed as she frantically rubs between her legs while tearing her kimono off. Her foster father is swearing and grunting and sweating, saying filthy words as Jana's eyes roll up to her foster mother's contorted face. Jana loses consciousness as she watches herself.

Both dream episodes end without answers or reason for their appearance to me.

I don't know why I've learned of this boy Robert's death and this is a terrible way to find out. I have no connection to anyone called Jana and yet there was a neighbor girl by that name who, I'm told, went to live with her grandmother when she was only about eight.

There are things that none of us have answers to and in this case I don't want to look for answers. I just hope to rid myself of the dreams.

It has become stunningly obvious to me that I have gone too far and I am certain that at some point along the line of unexplainable experiences there is an edge, a precipice. Once you have arrived there you either totter over or you recover your mental balance and are able to return to what we call reality. I will, therefore, leave here with every intention of returning someday. It would be the understatement of my 80 plus years if I were to say that it has been unusual and broadening, but also numbing when it was never meant to be.

There is, undoubtedly, a logical explanation which could probably be arrived at through Gestalt and I am intrigued with the idea of so doing. At this moment in time, however, I will first try reasoning with myself.

I am growing accustomed to that.

.

EPISODE 8:

THE TEMPLARS, KINGS AND POPE

THE PAST TEN DAYS have been desperately jumbled and confusing. I have returned to my Shearwater flat in Kinsale; it's pouring rain and even the Irish are admitting it isn't what they classify as a "soft day." There is a gale off shore in the Atlantic and gathering strength to attack later in the afternoon. I question the reasons for even getting up this morning, but it's not the worst alternative and I need the time to revisit my values, or at least the basic ones.

I'm searching for some of the underlying tenets of faith and, just perhaps, I'm also searching for reasons to re-establish some of my childhood beliefs in Christianity. I am not a *snug man*, as is said here when referring to those lucky enough to be content with life as it supposedly is.

I need to do this. I was talking last summer to someone whom I have loved and respected all of my life and I was trying to arrive at an understanding of the logic of God leaving out so many unfortunate people if he sent Jesus to save them. Like a child, I asked it simply enough. What about all those who grew up with beliefs other than Christian? Since God was starting all over again with us after The Flood, why didn't He make it universal?

There was thunder and lightening in the voice of the man I asked. He said, "Do you believe in God?" I was dumb-struck. Was the underlying psychological cause of my question because I didn't know if I believed in God? That thought was instant in its insistence. I couldn't answer either him or myself. Freud would have probably said that it was the reason I had asked. I don't think I could agree with Freud if that is what he would have posited. One can get into all kinds of twisted and convoluted thinking trying to come up with an answer, but since it came up I have tried, not without difficulty all along the way, to do just that.

I do believe in a force I call God because I am not smart enough to not believe. Was it Whitman in his *Leaves of Grass*, who suggested he needed look no further than a blade of grass or himself to be assured of God's existence and magnificent power? It is like that with me and yet I am also inquisitive enough to try to come up with arguments against His institution: The Church. Not His Church, our church. This may take a while as I dig around. And, remember, if you will, I am just returned from a good few days at the Rigpa and some marvelous teachings.

To my knowledge, Buddhists have never been at issue with Christianity or any other religion. Factually, my teachers at Dzogchen Beara have repeatedly endorsed the idea that if you believe in God or Jesus, that's your business and they most assuredly have no argument against such beliefs. It's just that they don't themselves.

I think I'm the one with the problem of any Christian conflict being contrary to the word of God. I have no disagreement of any kind with all the benevolent work they have accomplished or the good they continue to do. For me, the problem is that the leaders of organized Christian religions have such intolerance toward non Christians. Everyone's belief other than theirs is wrong. Jewish, Muslim, Shinto, Hindu, or whatever they perceive is threatening to their own totalitarian system. I could cope with it if the basic reason was that they wanted everyone to adopt their beliefs, but it isn't that. They truly are threatened, never questioning themselves. I reason that it goes back to the early days of the Christian church, or the Church of Rome.

I am taken with the idea that the Knights Templar found something in their first crusades to Syria and later to Jerusalem so detrimental and condemning of the Catholic Church's doctrine that it very seriously threatened the entire structure. One or the other had to go and it wasn't the Pope's idea or the King of France's idea that they should change or step down. That leaves the Templars to be destroyed and the Crusades, or rather the term Crusade, must take on a new meaning and an inverted purpose.

The original Templar Order was made up of soldier-monks bound by religious vows of poverty, chastity, and obedience who were engaged in a religious war in the Holy Land. They perceived a call to their destiny of protecting

Christians on pilgrimages to Jerusalem. Somewhere down the time-line the French government came to the conclusion that these men were no soldier-monks, but wealthy magicians. Though sworn to poverty, they were indeed wealthy through land grants from the church for their mercenary duties.

If you read all the research done and logically presented in *The Holy Blood and the Holy Grail,* you have to be fairly convinced that this terribly secret organization dating back to the days of the Crusades did find something to upset the Catholic Church back in Rome. And, it wasn't just one thing, it was a whole series of cover-up killings, wars, early Inquisitions, and obstructions sponsored by the church which should cause one to wonder just how much truth they have actually been telling the past 2000 plus years.

In fact it would seem very little truth has been told.

Dante Alighieri, the poet, believed the plot against the Templars was nothing less than greedy confiscation by the government of their land and money. Some of the later thinkers of the Enlightenment, while themselves adapting the Gnostic premise, thought these men were anti-Christs who had worked their way into the power structure of the Medieval Church with the purpose of destroying it from within. That the Medieval Church had become an evil institution is well documented and therein lay the never ending argument against any organized religion.

It is not the churches, or the states which are inherently evil; it is the people who have taken over their governance who turn the intrinsic power both inward and outward for their personal purposes.

If the Templars had truly set out to cleanse the church

from within and to destroy its ignominious irreverence, they never said so. They either remained virtually silent by sworn choice or they refused to disavow that purpose and thus promoted their destruction. By not making their case known they left unchallenged the charges of mystical or occult powers brought against them by the Church. Accordingly, this group of uneducated but dedicated soldiers had suddenly become enlightened seers who suddenly had a House of Wisdom at their fingertips and could paralyze humanity in a wizard's flash. Only the church and the French government could stop them. Together, the two of them must have been frightened silly by their own propaganda and it became a truly Gothic horror – a visionary heterodoxy unparalleled in its time.

Countless stories emanated from the accusations, some of which were attached to the Templars themselves and some of which were derived from the mysticism the charges created. The actual charges against the Templars in the papal decree of 1308 are so fantastical that Goebell and Himmler could have learned from them and perhaps they did. As it happens, the charges of mysticism and occult powers have a substantial enough base in the many religious revelations given us. There are the loaves and fishes, the water to wine and the whole genre isn't unique to Biblical stories. My own master, Padmasambhava, could fly, produce instant knowledge and was lotus born. Every other faith based operation on the face of the earth has made startling claims. One has to wonder a bit.

My continuing interest, however, lies in the full circle of the Templar mission. Urban II, the Pope in 1095, wanted to recapture Jerusalem which had fallen to the sword of Islam in 638 AD. He also wanted to force together the Eastern and Western strains of Christianity. To do so he launched the First Crusade and it gained control of Jerusalem in 1099 under the armies of Godefroy de Bouillon of Flanders. Urban died that year and after that those wishing to gain status made a pilgrimage there. They were protected by Christian soldiers along the route to the Holy Land and while they were worshiping there. In 1118, at Charentay, Hugues de Payne and eight other knights took the vows to the brotherhood devoted to Christ and with the purpose of protecting the pilgrims and the Holy Sepulcher. These were the first Templars.

Their first quarters were in King Baldwin's palace, which itself had been built on the site of King Solomon's Temple and was connected to the destroyed al Aqsa Mosque. Their horses were kept in the area allotted by the cannons of the Holy Sepulcher. The anomaly of the love-thy-enemy church and the killer-knights was likely doomed from the beginning, not because of the dichotomy, but because of the power likeness.

Paradoxically, the Knights Templar became the purifier and the Catholic Church of Rome and Byzantium became the killers. The Templars, as they grew in numbers and military power, also grew to be endorsed in their purpose throughout Europe. The stronger they grew, the more apprehensive became the officers of the church and horror of horrors, the very feudal system supported by the church and run by the kings, found common cause with the emperors thereabouts. The church had created the threat to its own undoing.

Scholars over the years have written most learned treatises, papers, dissertations and books on the workings of the Templars. They cover the Holy Grail theory, the rules of the Order, their admitted beliefs and even their diet and the diet of their horses. We all know what the Knights Templar wore and we know of his bravery. Alongside are the journals of alchemy, secret touchstones of primal knowledge and black enlightenment. They were, accordingly, far more esoteric than any mere monk or warrior could ever become in so short a time period.

Where did they come from and what was the true purpose of the Templars? What they came to realize whilst in Jerusalem was that Jesus as the Christ was a phenomenon the church was controlling by interpretive teaching to continue the mastery of the masses in cooperation with the kings. What the Templars discovered was the cosmic Christ and not the human revelation of God's rules of conduct. What they ran into was Gnosticism.

Briefly, most Gnostics considered themselves to be Christians, but some sects assimilated only minor Christian elements into a body of non-Christian Gnostic texts. Most Gnostic sect's beliefs diverged sharply from those of the majority of Christians in the early church and they were considered heretics. The term Gnosticism is derived from the Greek word *gnosis* ("revealed knowledge"). The Gnostics wrote apocryphal Gospels (such as the Gospel of Thomas and the Gospel of Mary) to substantiate their claim that the risen Jesus told his disciples the true, Gnostic interpretation of his teachings: Christ, the divine spirit, inhabited the body of the man Jesus and did not die on the cross, but ascended to the divine realm from which he had come (The Cosmic Christ). The Gnostics thus rejected the atoning suffering and death of Christ and the resurrection of the body. They also rejected other literal and traditional interpretations of the Gospels.

This was too close to the Jewish belief of Messianic deliverance. The Bible itself often revealed a living Christ who was involved with the creation of the earth and the universe as in John 8:58 and one who goes on living into eternity as in Matthew 28:20. The Christ as a cosmic being was to the Templars a magnificent force for good. The church they served was an infinitesimal, corrupt, self serving Philistinistic structure determined to control the Christ through Jesus. They were stuck in time. The cosmic Christ is a highly evolved being capable of empowering evolutionary changes to our further development. The Templars probably saw the Christ as hope, salvation and a theocratic escape from human religious constricts. Yet, so powerful was the Medieval Church that it drove them first underground, then to destruction. The church had won the battle, but the war goes on. The deadly foe was Gnostic to some, truth to others.

The Templars created intricate rules and practices in a web of both belief and camouflage. Perhaps what they never got to develop was the documentation of what now exists in the *Nag Hammadi Library*, a compilation of the Gnostic texts and scriptures which they had discovered. The church obviously knew about these discoveries made by the Templars and they had then attack the "Gnostic foul practices." The false etymology used by the church supporting writers had massed the Templars, the Jews, Gnostics, and heretics together as enemies of Christianity. They portrayed them through forgery and avarice as having denounced Jesus and as successors to the Gnostic Ophites in so doing. They even claimed the Holy Grail itself was Gnostic in origin and continued with Druidic religion.

The condemnations continued long after the Order had been destroyed, connecting perceived Gnostic beliefs and practices in classic literature, the arts and music, the theatre and even sinister androgynous beings. The lack of validity betrays their fear of historical truth of Gnostic writings.

Simultaneously, as if the Templars weren't enough of a problem, there was the growth of the Manicheans. A Persian called Manes was a mystic of recognizable status who espoused Gnostic tendencies. The early Gnostics believed in the basic doctrine that is dualism. There existed two creative forces: God created the spiritual world and a lower order created the material world. God is good, Satan is bad. Manes was initiated into the teachings of the Mysteries of Mithraism. He was also interested in the teachings of esoteric Judaism which became the Cabala. He thought that Jesus was neither the unique son of God nor the provider of salvation. Jesus was here to show the way. The Christ was within him, but the Christ is in all human beings. This Manichean thinking was influential in the Byzantine world and was being spread to France.

Here was another job for the Crusaders who weren't just to stop the Muslims, but to destroy the heresy of Gnostic/ Manichean believers. The church had to re-empower Jesus as Christ and so Manichaeism had to be eradicated. Fortunately or unfortunately for them, the Zoroastrians of Persia found Manes a bit too much and crucified him before the Roman Catholic church could mete out its justice.

As the Gnostics believed Christ had the power to show

evolutionary growth they saw the need for changes as they became more knowledgeable. They came to believe in the realization of one's divinity through inner revelations rather than the mastery of a given doctrine. This was very upsetting to the church who felt threatened by reason and logic, or more appropriately, thinking.

Again, perhaps what suddenly made the Templars so smart was the idea that they had found in their rummaging around in Solomon's grounds, evidence of the existence of the true Christ as interpreted by Gnostic scripture. Dualism didn't die with the Templars. It was revived to some degree through the Enlightenment, but the heterodoxy of dualism promoted in the writings of the Enlightenment period ignored the dualist promise of transcendent escape. It got examined into submission again.

As with a lot of things, over examination creates false interpretation. "Maybe this is what they meant" syndromes appear, witness Madame Blavatsky who wrote:

"Ialdabaoth, the creator of the material world, was made to inhabit the planet Saturn according to the Ophites. From Ialdabaoth emanate six spirits who respectively dwell with their father in the seven planets... These seven planets are identical with the Hindu *Sapta-lokas*, the seven places or spheres, or the superior and inferior worlds; for they represent the kabalistic seven spheres. With the Ophites they belong to the lower spheres. The monograms of these Gnostic planets are also Buddhistic, the latter differing, albeit slightly from those of the usual astrological "houses."

It can be said that anything or nothing is as it appears, depending upon the viewer.

What we do principally know is taken from the indictment that, "Great scandal has been generated against the Order in the minds of important people, including those of kings and princes, and indeed among the whole Christian people." The real struggle was between the power of the Crown of France and the Pope and the Templars were to pay the ultimate price.

The Templars were sent to kill the rogue lion, but instead became the larger lion and an extremely dangerous one. Faced with the truth, the learned but greedy-for-greater-power men of the church knew what must be done. In order to keep their power and their pact with the kings of Europe they must kill the lion themselves.

Such evil would not stay unrecognized and the Gnostic pronouncements would eventually be found in the reform brought by the Protestants.

Whatever I eventually conclude, the fact does remain in my mind, and firmly so, there is Buddha in all of us. Just as the Gnostics with the Christ. There is overall, a unity of thought there.

The work of Michael Baigent, Richard Leigh, and Henry Lincoln is monumental in its thoroughness, its dogged research and persistence in keeping the goal before them, and, I think, the truth always in mind. *The Holy Blood and the Holy Grail* is a fantastic series of revelations and, to me, their quotation of Carl Jung, taken from 'The Undiscovered Self', *Collected Works,* vol. 10 (1956) p. 266 and appearing in their Conclusions and Portents For The Future poses the correct summarial question:

"But if, for instance, the statement that Christ arose from the dead is to be understood not literally but symbolically, then it is capable of various interpretations that do not conflict with knowledge and do not impair the meaning of the statement. The objection that understanding it symbolically puts an end to the Christian hope of immortality is invalid, because long before the coming of Christianity mankind believed in a life after death and therefore had no need of the Easter event as a guarantee of immortality. The danger that a mythology understood too literally, and as taught by the Church, will suddenly be repudiated lock, stock and barrel is today greater than ever. I must, therefore, ask the question. Is it not time that the Christian mythology, instead of being wiped out, was understood symbolically for once?"

It somehow follows that the absolutism of the church and government would reach infectiously into the New World. Just as greed accommodated power in Europe, so it was deployed and developed in the lives of the native pagan peoples through the colonial system. The self proclaimed piety for the good of mankind was never any more evident than in North and South America, nor had the inherent training in inhumanity ever been so acute as during the years of the Inquisition.

How reflective it has been of the earliest of interpretation of God's will where I had glimpsed it in the stories of the Flood. On the one side was the Biblical practice of examining and marching along the path of fear to achieve salvation and the Gilgamesh willingness to forgive ignorance.

Now it was the time of the Spanish, bathed in blood and the righteous ungodliness of self-congratulation in their victory over evil heresy and with unquestionable strength. I am again entering into the arena of what is right and wrong and I am looking specifically at what came to be called Mexico and her people. It comes to mind that my prolonged interest in what is right and what is wrong has shaded my conclusions and the drama has, by premature denouement, impaired the outcome. I most sincerely hope that is not the case. I am trying to deal with manipulation of some well meant people by those in charge of meting out that precious and scarce commodity, eternal life. It should not be confused with the espousement of truth, ever. Here we will be looking at the excrement and not the golden bowl in which it floats.

To view ancient Mexico through European eyes is to view it as a barbaric land, but with the monuments, art and culture it compares with other civilizations of the Nile River, the Tigris and the Euphrates or of Hindustan. Their accomplishments stem from the earliest Toltecs in the 7th century AD through the Chichemecs, the Acolhuans and finally the Mexicans in the early 14th century. Their government was an elective monarchy based on the strength of treaty agreements between the Aztec and Tezcucan nations.

Their justice system dealt heavily with capital crime. Likewise, bribery or collusion to obfuscate justice meant death. A sentence when passed was illustrated dramatically by a line traced by an arrow across a portrait of the accused. The king presided in capital sentencing. Even the killing of a slave was a capital offense. Prodigals who squandered their patrimony were severely punished. Death of a slave owner usually gave the unfortunates their freedom. The Aztec code displayed the severity and ferocity of a hardened people, familiar with the blood and relying on physical rather than moral means for the correction of proven evils.

The government was supported by a tax system and by tribute. Communication between regions was carried out by means of post houses, two leagues apart. Surprise, surprise, the public honors were directed by priests supported by soldiers, much like Egypt. The top god was the God of War and the king and princes rewarded their supporters through a lower form of knighthood. Civil and religious policy was nearly homogeneous and mythology was the poetry of their religion.

Such is the nature of human need that the mythology becomes self indulgent. To do so, the priests used allegory and gave their deities grotesque concepts of ferocious retribution. At the same time, they recognized a supreme Creator and Lord of the universe and knew him to be omnipresent, perfect and omniscient as well as invisible and incorporeal.

So, these were the heathens the Christian Church; never mind its own history, set out to free or perhaps conversely, to enslave. The conquerors would encounter the terrible Huitzilopotichli, the patron deity of the Mexican nation. This god was born of a woman, who, while at a temple, saw a bright colored ball of feathers floating in front of her. She took it and placed it in her bosom and found herself pregnant. Huitzilopoticehli was born fully armed with a shield in his left hand and a spear in his right. His fierce head was adorned with green feathers. Here recalls Minerva and the chief deities from Northern India beyond the Ganges. Christ was born of a virgin as were the Fohi of China and the Shaka of Tibet. It is said the Jesuits in China were distressed to find the mythology of the people predating the Vigo Deipara and I am reminded of Atisha's 11th century account of the history of Jesus in India for 18 years.

The Mexican mythology surrounding Quetzalcoatl, the god of air, during his residence on earth gave instructions to the people on growing crops, working with metal and governance. The other gods grew jealous of him and forced him to leave the country. He left from the Gulf of Mexico, heading for a land known as Tlapallan in a magic skiff made of snake skins. Interestingly, Quetzalcoatl was tall, was white skinned, had long dark hair and he promised to return. This brief description of a benevolent deity whose reappearance was so looked forward to would bode ill for his believers and greatly benefit the Spaniards when Hernando Cortes came wading ashore in 1519.

Custom follows custom: religion develops cultural design. In the Aztec way of religious life when a person died they were dressed in the costume of their tutelary god. Pieces of colored paper were scattered over the body, slaves were sacrificed, the cremation took place, and ashes placed in an urn and kept in his house. Roman Catholic, Muslim and Tartar each had near similar practices.

Their children were named in a ceremony in which the holy water was sprinkled over the child's lips and breast and prayers were offered to wash away the sins given it before the beginning of the earth. These were the unwashed the Spanish were compelled to convert.

The many brutal practices of the Aztecs lived by in law and by the nature of their society were, indeed, ungodly, but the European world was every bit as uncaring. The difference was in the gods they worshiped.

Just as in the Catholic Church, the temple priests — thousands of them — taught choral music, saw to the education of their youth, arranged the festivals and ceremonies and heard confessions. The later, however, was a one time offering and if one repeated their confessed sin it was unforgivable. As could be expected, the confession usually took place later in life when many sins had been already been stored up. A certificate of confession served as a pardon in place of legal punishment. Girls could be placed in training for the exercise of sacerdotal functions, save that of sacrifice.

The practice of human sacrifice was not put in use by the Aztecs until the early 14th century. There were incredible festivals to honor the god Tezcatlipoca, who ranked second only to their Supreme Being. A handsome young man was selected, cleaned, groomed, provided with four beautiful young bed partners, revered and worshiped for a year. He was then taken to the temple, ascended the pyramid, stretched out face up on the sacrificial stone, his chest slit open with a flint-like stone knife and his beating heart removed, then cast at the feet of the deity to whom the temple was dedicated.

European visitors, afoul of the priests, met the same fate after suffering tortures of the most intrusive kind. Captive enemies, sacrificed in the thousands, were an annual event and in 1486 a massacre of over 100,000 took place. This hugely outnumbered those burned at the stake or otherwise executed in Europe during the period of the Inquisition, but the same purpose was accomplished by eliminating the non-believers or those wrongly accused of being non-believers. In Mexico it was an offering to the gods. In

Europe it was murder, in many cases, of innocent persons for the purpose of cleansing the population of heretics. Mercy was not in the hearts of the priests of Mexico or the Pope of the Holy Catholic Church. Human sacrifice is not considered degrading to the victim; instead it was thought to be ennobling and a most glorious death. Each year during the 16th Century Inquisition in Europe thousands were destroyed by arming brother against brother and in so doing set themselves backward and apart from the Bible. The one great difference was the cannibalism in the Aztec world, dictated by their religious code. Strangely, the Toltecs, their antecedents, never stained an altar with human blood, yet another example of how far organized religion can be blamed for the heinous actions against its fellowman.

The measure of a culture is recorded in its art, particularly its religious art. The Flemish and the Italian Renaissance period are marvels of the emotional interpretation of the teachings of Jesus and the Biblical word of God. The church became the patron provider to the depth such talents could portray. The Russian Orthodox and the Byzantine churches, though separate from Rome, continued to produce prodigious quantities of historic scenes.

In Mexico the picture writing of the Aztecs was not limited to religious rules and stories. It incorporated their laws, their domestic economy, tribute roles, mythology, their rituals political views and calendars. It was their art and their literature, done with great care and with a colorful beauty. They used cotton, animal skins, a fabric made of the aloe leaves called maguey, a type of paper as soft as and even more beautiful than the Egyptian papyrus.

The Spaniards, in their zealous ignorance and determined to wash the Aztec souls, looked upon these book like collections with suspicion and assumed them to be dangerous symbols which must be eradicated. Don Juan Zumarraga, First Bishop of Mexico, gathered them from every corner, every bibliotheca and every depository. He had them piled high in the market place of Tlateloco and burned them in a replication of what Archbishop Ximenes had done with the magnificent Arabic manuscripts in Granada following the expulsion of the Moors in 1492. So complete was the destruction of the Mexican hieroglyphics that when Boturini traveled through the country in the late 1700's he could find no one who could read the few remaining.

The good will and intentions of Ferdinand and Isabella was never inherited by their successor, Charles V. His Flemish background and the sycophants who accompanied him to power were to be the near ruination of a country whose colonial intentions and government had been that of benign despotism. They simply didn't understand anything about decency, respect or duty.

Born in the same year, 1485, as that "infernal beast," *the false heretic, Martin Luther,* Hernando Cortes was destined to become the scourge of the Spanish Empire abroad in Mexico. His spirit directed him toward the adventure of the military and had he not fallen from a ladder while climbing to the bedroom of a lady, he would have sailed with Don Nicholas de Ovando, the successor to Christopher Columbus for the New World two years earlier than he eventually did. Unfortunately for Mexico, he lived through a series of debacles in the service of ship's captains, army commanders, engagements to marry and the

threat of ending his days tilling the soil rather than searching for gold and carrying the cross through the lands of
the Aztecs. His exploits in Hispaniola are legendary with
myriad escapes, sanctuary, contrition and reconciliation
with his commander, the Governor of Cuba, Velasquez. In
reward, it would seem, he was chosen to pursue the riches
of Honduras. He was entrusted with an armada of discovery, trade and the conquest which departed for Cape Saint
Antonio, the point for the ships rendezvous.

There were 11 ships, the largest just 100 tons. On shore
the mustering showed Cortes to have 110 marines, 553 soldiers of whom 32 were cross bowmen, and 13 were har-
quebusiers. There were also 200 Indians and a few Indian
women. He had 10 heavy guns, four smaller ones and a lot
of ammunition. He also had 16 horses, his most valuable
asset in the support of such a bold adventure. He addressed
his troops and assured them their cause was just; the enemy
was infidels and their protection and purpose, The Cross.

The symbolic use of The Cross was given with full en-
dorsement by the Church; a mass was said and the fleet was
placed under the protection of St. Peter, the patron saint of
Cortes. They sailed for the coast of Yucatan to convert the
heathens and just maybe become incredibly wealthy if not
dead.

The fleet was scattered by storms and Cortes was last to
land at Cozumel where the earlier arriving ships had put
in. One of the captains, Pedro de Alvarado, had sacked the
temples. Cortes was outraged and restored the loot while
sending two natives, loaded with trinkets, to spread the
words of apology and the peaceful intent of their presence.

His first gesture brought near instant results and he was

soon enough credited and identified as being the vanquished white god, now returned. In Cortes' travels throughout the island he was soon to find a cross of stone and lime. It was in actuality the symbol of the rain god. To the expedition, however, it meant that it was a divine assurance that Christianity had once been visited upon the race and must be restored.

Here, then, was a new crusade and they fell to the conversion with an enthusiastic sword; a certain argument where only the tongue would fail. A true and high mission for the soldier of The Cross. To die for the Lord was the creed of the Castilian knight. It was word de jur, la palabra del mundo.

That is it was but for one man: father Bartolome de Olmeda, who was to remain with the army through the whole expedition and whose wise charity and kindness remained true to the word of God. His duty, however, along with that of licentiate Juan Diaz, was to prevail upon the pagans to renounce their beliefs and to allow the idols to be destroyed. This was a ridiculous request and could only bring revenge were it to happen.

Cortes, a man of action not diplomacy, had the images torn down the stairs of the great temple and an alter was constructed in the image of the Virgin Mary and Christ was placed over it and mass said. While appalled by such action, the natives pragmatically recognized the weakness of their own gods against the guns and cannon of the Spanish and agreed that the sword was indeed, mighty.

Convinced of the conversion, Cortes prepared to take his mission to the mainland and just perchance enrich himself materially along the way. The small fleet departed, but returned to port with a serious leak in one of the ships. This was Providence portrayed as along came a canoe with a man named Jeronimo de Aguilar, a survivor of a ship wreck eight years previous. He had survived in the jungles of the interior and had heard of the arrival of Cortes through the native grapevine. His was a miraculous survival and he was to become an invaluable priestly aide to Cortes. He was aided even more by Marina, a native of Coatzacualco who had been sold by her mother into slavery and had been presented to Cortes by the cacique of Tabasco. She spoke the dialects needed for translation to Aguilar, who then could speak in Castilian. So far, so good.

This was not to be the case after his meeting with the powerful emperor, Montezuma, the name the conquest's historian Bernal Diaz had given him for some reason. From 1510 forward to 1519 there had been a series of uncommon occurrences which the natives concluded were connected to Quetzalcoatl, the god who had promised to return. An earthquake centered in Lake Tezuco, an unexplainable fire in the great temple and the resurrection of Montezuma's sister, Papantzin, four days after her burial to warn him of the ruination and fall of his empire.

Montezuma was distressed to see Quetzalcoatl's prophecy being fulfilled however wrongfully, by the appearance of Cortes. He chose the wrong welcome and rather than having Cortes destroyed on the spot, he sent him gifts of great fortune while telling him to stay away from his capital. He had thereby shown his weakness as well as the workmanship of the gold artisans. The Spaniards were stunned, but the message sent was clear. *Get out. Stay out and go home.* Cortes smiled and moved closer.

The Spanish formed an armed alliance with the powerful Totanic nation, sworn enemies of their conquerors, the Aztecs of Montezuma. Cortes announced to their chief he had been sent by his God to abolish inhuman worship. The cacique replied that his gods of sun and rain were good enough for them, but that his people were being enslaved and scarified in huge numbers by the Aztecs. He also said he could muster thousands and that Tlascala tribute could and would do the same. Whatever the personal purposes of Cortes were, the mission of conversion remained. The methods of subordination were brutal.

It was soon apparent that Cortes, by his merciless actions, was not Quetzalcoatl who had returned, but a foreign demon. Their fate was not freedom, but subjugation, the destruction of their religion and death. And, all was not well within the Spanish forces and severe retribution was taken against those who plotted against Cortes in a plan to force return, if not to Spain, at least to the safety of Valasques in Cuba. A priest was involved, Juan Diazo. He was pardoned as a member of the church, but the others were executed or whipped senseless. Cortes ordered the ships of his fleet sunk. There would be no return. His public excuse for the scuttling was that they had become un-seaworthy and as such of no further use.

In an incredibly short span of time Cortes had left Cuba, entered Mexico, made useless the pagan temples along the way, entered into revolutionary cause with two native tribes, destroyed the myth of Quetzalcoatl, became extraordinarily wealthy and aggravated the most powerful emperor, Montezuma. He had also built a town, freed the ship wrecked Christian and obtained the important guide and translator, Marina.

Their march toward Montezuma's capital city continued and his crusade of conversion along the way through
Cempoalla and into Tlascalan lands where an army covering six square miles and numbering 150,000 awaited them.
Obviously, the Christian army was not welcomed with the
open arms once promised. Relentlessly Cortes drove his
army forward with the admonition and reminder that they
fought under the banner of the Cross.

The events of conversion en route continued into the
capital with the arrest of caciques and priest of the Totanacs.
Fifty soldiers tore down the huge idols and rolled them
down the steps of the pyramids, then burned them. An alter was erected, a huge cross garlanded with flowers raised
and the former Indian priests led the procession carrying
images of the Virgin Mary and lighted candles.

In the city of Cholula, the Spanish found a huge pyramid where Quetzalcoatl had taught as well as finding mysterious similarities of the Incarnation and Trinity. Here,
also, Marina discovered a conspiracy against the army and
Cortes entrapped the caciques and forced their admis-
sion of their intended treachery. On order hundreds of
Cholulans assembled in the square and were massacred.
The Tlascalan allies then attack the town. The Cholulans
who had escaped the massacre fled to the pyramid and ended their lives by plunging from the top. Such mass killings
by the Spanish were a part of the discipline of the church.
Religious infidelity was a sin to be punished with death
and eternal fires of damnation. It was the creed of the
Church of Rome under which code any and all heathen
lands and people became the property of the Holy See. In

the process Cortes caused more than a hundred chiefs to be impaled or roasted at the stake and while doing so repeated a bit of poetry inspired by the mad Nero:

> Mira Nero de Tarpeya,
> A Roma como se ardia.
> Grios clan ninos y viejos,
> Y el de nada se dolia

These were the duties assigned by the Pope.

The beauty and grandeur or the architecture Cortes and army found in the capital were overwhelming. The museums, palaces, the Royal household and Montezuma's life style were beyond anything they could have ever imagined in so pagan a place. Cortes was, however, a soldier of the Church first and as a soldier was cautious in their vastly outnumbered presence. He was less than assured of his safety when viewing the large block of jasper with its convex surface which raised the breast of those to be sacrificed for convenience of the priest enjoined to perform the diabolical task of removing the still beating heart.

The killings continued as Montezuma refused conversion. The hard work of the Catholic Church continued in unrelenting intensity. So cruel was their treatment of Montezuma and so insistent on his acceptance that he finally lost the fierce spirit that had maintained him and he accepted Spanish dominance after they had executed his officers and priests. Yet Montezuma warned that his gods would prevail and he questioned why Cortes would continue with his self destruction.

A nation and a culture had been destroyed, its riches robbed and the church ruled supreme. The Spanish established an empire abroad in Mexico and in Peru, along with the Portuguese who between them split the world in two with a papal agreement.

When the church has conquered, who is left to forgive them?

EPISODE 9:

SCARCE ELEMENTS
OF TRUTH

IN MY TIME AWAY from Dzogchen Beara and with library resources available I have become increasingly convinced that the Christian church, both Catholic and Protestant, have deliberately perpetrated untruths for centuries about Jesus to hold their power. When I try to talk to leaders of any branch of Christianity about the facts denying their position and its basic truths, they continue to defend it on the basis of faith. One cannot deny that power. I can only ask why they refuse to examine the evidence even in the most cursory manner or allow themselves the honesty of confession, which is, after all, a self declared cleansing of the soul. For them, blindness appears to be more comfortable.

Within the evidence available is the logic of truthful presentation. The question is always asked. Why set out to

refute Jesus as the Christ? In all of the cases I have considered there was never any intent to prove or disprove the
Christian belief – only the desire to do the hard work of
finding what parts are true and what parts are not. I leave
the stories to the researchers and can only deal with the
summary and conclusion.

What the Templars discovered was what the Gnostics
knew all along. Jesus did not die on the cross. In the *Nag
Hammadi Scrolls*, in the Second Treatise of the Great Seth,
Jesus speaks of the event and of Simon of Cyrene, who died
in crucifixion instead. He says,

"I did not succumb to them as they had planned… And
I did not die in reality, but in appearance, lest I be put to
shame by them… For my death which they think happened
[happened] to them in their error and blindness, since they
nailed their man into their death… It was another, their
father, who drank the gall and vinegar, it wasn't I. They
struck me with the reed; it was another, Simon, who bore
the cross on his shoulder. It was another upon whom they
placed the crown of thorns.… And I was laughing at their
ignorance."

Jesus, thereupon, escaped with his wife, Mary Magdalene,
from their wedding of Cana, to France. Their followers and
their progeny became the Merovingians, a race of people
who later assumed leadership in the ruling families of their
adopted country. With such evidence the case against the
church becomes even more personally desperate. With this
particular set of facts laid out it is the hierarchy of the church
who has become the heretics and guilty of the greatest
crime imaginable: the use of the Holy teachings for human
power. In so doing, they have condemned themselves to

samsara, the ocean of suffering, unendurable and unbearably intense. As in the Four Causes of Buddhist renunciation, "Unalterable are the laws of karma, cause and effect cannot be escaped." In the words of the Christian teaching, "As ye sow, so shall ye reap."

It occurs to me that if the Buddhists were not so loving, kind and gentle, they would have made issue of these Christian fallacies. That is not their nature or the intent, however, and as every person is responsible for their lives, only the individual can stop the cycle of *samsara*; only through becoming a decent person can it end. The meditation practice is dedicated through the Four Immeasurable and the motivation is established with that dedication:

> By the power of the truth of this practice,
> May all sentient beings enjoy happiness,
> and the causes of happiness,
> Be free from suffering, and the causes of suffering,
> May they never be separated from the great
> happiness devoid of suffering,
> And may they dwell in the great equanimity
> that is free from attachment and aversion.

How beautifully simple it seems. How extraordinarily different it must be for Christians to accept The Christ, the cosmic Christ, without Jesus upon whom they have believed for 2000 years! But if one does believe in truth it is that simple. One only has to look at the Three Noble Principles as taught by Soygol Rinpoche in his book, *The Tibetan Book of Living and Dying* to learn that the process is so pure that it can appear daunting. The term "practice" for meditation is just that: It takes a lot of practice, but it will come, given time and attention.

Meditation can be merely a way of becoming quiet – to be relaxed and at peace. It can also be much different and it can become a powerful cause for enlightenment of yourself and others. They call it Good in the Beginning, Good in the Middle and Good at the End.

In brief, Good at the Beginning is the basic awareness that we all possess – the buddha nature – and that is to realize it is to be free of ignorance and to end our suffering. In so doing, we help ourselves and others.

Good in the Middle is the mind set with which we are inspired to be non-grasping and to bring us to the realization that all things are illusory and empty. Again, that there is nothing of value in this life which will go with us when we die other than our goodness.

Good in the End is the closing dedication of meditation by earnestly praying, "May whatever merit that comes from this practice go toward the enlightenment of all beings; may it become a drop in the ocean of the activity of all the buddhas in their tireless work for the liberation of all beings." In a practical way, the merit of dedication is for peace and happiness.

That this last, Good in the End, may sound similar to the benediction of Lutheran service is no coincidence. All religions are dedicated to the same thing and all Christian purpose is predicated on the same premise. The teacher, Jesus, was adamant in those lessons and the Beatitudes are directed in the same manner. All moral teachings are of the same seminal purport.

Buddha characterized his life before enlightenment as being in jail and ignorance was his jailer. In his enlightenment, Buddha realized that the key to ending the misery of *samsara* was to bring the mind home to its true nature through meditation. Meditation is to attune the mind to an open and sky like attitude, yet remain in the present and grounded. It is to achieve a new operating system for the mind to be comfortable and secure, away from the "normal' confusion.

In this state we become free of all cares and concerns and worry. We let them go. All the scattered problems which obviate our natural serenity are allowed to leave us and we bring the mind home. That "home" is our central being where our natural buddha being lives eternally.

This bringing the mind home is also called the practice of mindfulness and creates the space and attitude of Calm Abiding. We begin to settle and we also begin to understand ourselves; we become friends with ourselves. We discover that lessens our negativity, our acquired aggression, our pain and we can see an end to our mental suffering and frustration of dealing with our daily lives.

These acquired problems cannot be dismissed, but they can be viewed with less suppressive effort and by simply accepting their existence. This mindfulness, this acceptance reduces the tension of constantly fighting them. It begins to defuse them and you begin to feel well in your being; well in your own skin. The release then comes and you begin to become at ease. It is therapeutic and healing and it costs nothing.

The practice will help reveal your natural goodness as well and it releases kindness. It is the fundamental Good Heart and brings great peace and non aggressive attitude. Nyoshul Khenpo wrote a poem which encapsulates this wisdom:

Rest in natural peace
This exhausted mind
Beaten helpless by karma
and neurotic thought,
Like the restless fury of the pounding wave.
In the infinite ocean of samsara,
Rest in natural peace

It has everything to do with creating the correct inner environment. The method is a means, but it is not the meditation itself. It is being able to push the boat away once you've reached the shore. Meditation is nothing more or less than getting used to the practice of meditation and one becomes a part of the practice.

While meditating in the company of others one also becomes aware that there are those whose habits of positive or physical difficulties must adapt. It is recommended that we have our eyes open, as well as the mouth slightly open as though saying "ah", but I continue to find that I am quicker to the objectivity if I keep my eyes closed as well as my mouth. In watching the breath, too, I have devised what for me is an excellent process whereby I "roll" my breathing which means I combine what U Pandita calls observing the rise and fall of the abdomen with the breathing. I can rhythmically do both and the intake of the breath rolls through the top of my mouth and is naturally rolled out. It is very helpful and satisfying to have my own way.

When these fellow meditators are asked by the teachers if, when, and how long they meditate the replies are, to me, surprisingly varied. It ranges from "twice a day," which is my preference, to "once a day," "once a week," "once a month," to "when I need it."

I was most surprised at the brief periods given to meditation, with the majority saying "two or three minutes." I am given to wondering how busy everyone must be that they can only give "two or three" minutes a day to themselves. I am so fortunate that I can, if I wish, take at least 15 minutes, each morning and evening toward Calm Abiding.

I have one new friend, a barrister from Dublin who has another barrister friend, also a practicing meditator, who calls him every morning at 7 a.m. to tell him it's time to meditate. We now call that "dial a Buddha."

Another participant at the Heart of Wisdom presentation admitted to going for days, sometimes weeks, without meditating. Then when he did begin again he would practice for half an hour three, four or even five times a day. Was he driven by guilt? He didn't think so. Was he just catching up? No, he didn't feel a need to catch up. It was my amused conviction that I had met my first binge Buddhist.

Whatever the case, the need is ever present to develop an open, compassionate, and spacious attitude toward emotional interruptions as the practice is carried out. It is said that we "must neither follow thoughts nor invite them; be like the ocean looking at its own waves, or the sky gazing down at the clouds that pass through it."

There is an established fact that between old thoughts and new ones, a gap appears. It is this gap period in which the rigpa becomes apparent. This is the knowledge of knowledge and is best exemplified as the meditation learning experience by the story of a student of the great teacher, Jamyang Khyentse, a man named Apa Pant. He, in the eastern tradition, kept asking his master over and over, "How does one meditate?" One day, while watching a "Lama Dance" in front of the Palace Temple in Gangtok, the master was again being pestered with, "How does one meditate?" and he replied that "When the past has ceased, and the future thought has not yet arisen, isn't there a gap?"

"Yes," said Apa Pant.

"Well, prolong it. That is meditation."

The whole purpose of meditation is to learn how to integrate the values of the practice with everyday life. People can meditate for years and still not be affected in their daily life. One would have to believe they haven't learned how the permeation can take place. We can find the beauty, the calm, the peace as we meditate, but then when the meditation is ended, if it is ended quickly, even abruptly with the something likened to, "Well, that's over with. Back to the grindstone!" and thus leaving it all behind us. We are advised to come out of the meditation slowly, bringing our subconscious intent with us. If we dedicate the practice properly, it is a relative matter. We can live the means of meditation and we can carry it over into the present.

As Soygal Rinpoche is quoted as saying, "To embody the transcendent is why we are here."

I am curious about people who develop and write words of wisdom on how to live a kind and thoughtful life. They expound endlessly on their discovery of the secret of life and for a few coins will help you to achieve the very same near state of euphoria. It seems they would like to see us all believe that they came onto their visionary wisdom as a result of hard work, soul searching and spiritual development within themselves. Sadly, they either have no fear of being discovered as plagiarists or they are willing to take the chance that their audience, their believers, their adherents and the public in general are too bewildered to realize the truth. If any of us takes the trouble to look more closely, we would quickly see their fraudulence. Every one of them got it from someone else, and more frequently than not it came from a simple religion or philosophy. As some wise person once said, "There is nothing new under the sun." The Old Testament, the Koran, or the teachings of Buddha is the basis of all.

And the pity is, in the desire to appear wise and prophet-like; they never give credit to the true source for fear of losing their ego poise. Yet, even more remarkable is the fact that, at least in the case of the Buddha/Buddhist practitioners, there are no complaints. It would seem they are happy enough that if it helps someone, even though there is nothing new, that's just fine.

When I first worked on the development of Creative Problem Solving with Dr. Bernice Bleedhorn, way back in 1975-76, I soon discovered another fact. There is no such thing as "original thought"; for that matter, nothing is original at all and never has been. Everything derives from something relative and therefore the fact that the enlightened Buddha had discovered the true source of all knowledge as being the truth of everything has always been there and he found that in the simplest of ways. An unbounded, limitless volume of universal knowledge is in all of us, just as is said there is a Buddha in all of us. This buddha mind exists and we are all in possession of it. What can be done is to find it.

Is it the perfect answer? No, as nothing is perfect so long as humans are involved.

While the focus of Buddhism has always been on oneself and on others, shunting egoistic pursuits and endeavoring to gain a better understanding of one's connection to all people and things, there is historical evidence of doctrinal fanaticism and feudalism in exploitive aggrandizement.

Michael Parenti, PhD, Centre for Research on Globalization, Canada, wrote a stunning article in the November, 2007 issue of Nexus magazine. He lists legendary battles waged by Buddhist kings; the battle between thousands of monks of the Chogye Buddhist sect in South Korea for control of the order. The winning stakes were for a $9.2 million budget and millions more in property plus the rights to appoint 1,700 monks to a variety of offices. Quoting Dr. Parenti, "As with any religion, squabbles between or within Buddhist sects are often fueled by the material corruption and personal differences of the leadership." He then asks the question, "But, what of Tibetan Buddhism? Is it not an exception to this sort of strife?" He says that many Buddhists maintain that, before the Chinese crackdown in 1959, Tibet was a spiritually orientated kingdom free from the egotistical lifestyle, empty materialism and corrupting vices that besets modern society.

Quite the contrary. Old Tibet was a good deal like Europe during the religious wars of Counterreformation and the first Dalai Lama was actually installed by the Chinese Army; the second Dalai Lama resembled the early Popes of the Catholic Church, with many mistresses, partying and led such a sybaritic life that he was murdered by his own priests. So were five other Dalai Lamas over the next 170 years. In 1660 the fifth Dalai Lama faced a rebellion by the rival Kagyu sect In Tang province. The Dalai Lama ordered the Mongul army to annihilate the rebels, "... like eggs smashed against the rocks...."

Later, in 1792, many of the rival Kagyu monasteries were confiscated and the monks were compelled to convert to the Dalai Lama's denomination. Members of this Gelug school were known as "Yellow Hats" and had a traditional prayer which was chanted as:

> Praise you violent god of the Yellow Hat teachings
> who reduces to particles of dust great beings,
> high officials and ordinary people
> who pollute and corrupt the Gelug doctrine

Economics is a potent driving force in all religions and until 1959 when the present Dalai Lama escaped to the west, most of the tillable land was owned either by the wealthy secular landlords or the rich theocratic lamas, worked by serfs. An example would be the Deprung monastary which owned 185 manors, 25,000 serfs, 300 great pastures and 16,000 herdsmen. The Dalai Lama lived in the 1,000 room, 14 storey Potala Palace.

The serfs were treated little better than slaves and were under a lifetime bond to work their master's land, secular or monastic. In return for their labor the overlords had no responsibility to his serfs. There were also slaves, usually domestic servants who owned nothing and their offspring were born to follow into slavery.

The theocracy's religious teachings taught that the poor and afflicted had brought their troubles upon themselves, "because of their wicked ways in previous lives..." The rich and powerful treated their good fortune as a reward for, and evidence of, virtue in their past and present lives.

In the 1960's, Stuart and Roma Gelder were traveling in Tibet and interviewed a former serf, Tsereh Wan Tuei, who had stolen two sheep belonging to a monastery. For this crime both of his eyes were gouged out and one of his hands was mutilated beyond use. He is no longer a Buddhist.

The history of the crushing acts of oppression is an extremely long and violent one. Partenti goes on to say that, "Whatever wrongs and new oppressions the Chinese introduced after 1959, they did abolish slavery and the Tibetan serfdom system of unpaid labor. They eliminated the many crushing taxes, started work projects and greatly reduced unemployment and beggary." He also reveals that the 14th Dalai Lama's annual payment from the CIA was $185,000 per year and that the Tibetan exile community was secretly pocketing $1.7 million a year. As with the pontiffs, the liberating movement underpinning the statements and releases from the Dalai Lama have supported the "inalienable and fundamental human rights" of the working people throughout the world and removed the traditional obstacles that have kept Tibetan nuns from receiving an education.

Parenti summarizes by saying, "Tibetan feudalism was cloaked in Buddhism, but the two are not to be equated. In reality, old Tibet was not a paradise lost. It was a retrograde, repressive theocracy of extreme privilege and poverty, a long way from Shangri-La."

What we need to recognize and know is that any and all religions and philosophies or scientific data can be and likely will be corrupted by the messenger. I will compare it to any dream that anyone has. It is never truly told as it actually happened.

And so, the white swans swim in the dark harbour beneath my open window.

EPISODE 10:

GOOD SCIENCE / COMMERCIAL SCIENCE

I THINK THAT PERHAPS trying to explain or to understand the complexities of life and death is just too overwhelming. We ponder and we profess, but what does it do in the very end of this space we call our lives? Perhaps I need to take some of the heavy findings of science and reduce their promises or threats with the teachings of Buddha and those who followed him. Even in doing so, the difference between Theravadan and Mahayan traditions, the Indian and the Tibetan, and the Zen can tend to move the inherent values into different perspectives.

I am inclined, first of all, to question the importance of our creation. What has been put forth is only theory; with that of the Big Bang being of no more importance than any of the others. The noted philosopher, Roderic Knowles, goes back beyond the Creation and credits emptiness or void before the beginning of the universe as the ground for all reality. No matter, as we think of it, not cosmic, not sub-atomic particles, just energy. This isn't the energy used scientifically, but a living, intelligent field of pure awareness.

Einstein called the void a field, saying that, "finally there is no place in this new kind of physics for both field and matter, for the field is the only reality."

One could be very happy just to leave it that. Science has its place, we can agree, but doesn't the threat of science cause us all to be more apprehensive and frightened than need be? We are constantly bombarded with the discoveries of science, these archeologists, those practitioners in the droning of new facts. Certainly, in the areas of medicine and chemistry there has been and perhaps always will be a need for research, but how has human life been improved by the knowledge that there is yet another theory being developed to prove that we all started with an explosion or that we, for that matter, all derive from one family deep in Africa? Nice to know? Perhaps it is so. Do we need to know? No, it means nothing.

The deeper man's penetration of the past, the shallower our lives become. Science separates the tangibles and the intangibles and often makes the outcome seem that man's conscience is of no true or measurable worth. I have heard on more than one occasion that, "If you cannot measure it, it doesn't exist." I have a deep and abiding feeling about that for I think pretty much that it is the opposite in many cases.

Only in the material world, not the living world, does everything have to be measured. I think the most important thing to be measured is man's worth and only the living conscience of man can measure that. I am most wearied with quotes, too. This world famous scientist in Berkley or London or Tokyo has made a startling pronouncement about how long his particular nanosecond is. Does it really matter? Mine is probably just as long as his is and I am over 80 years old. Does anything matter if that quote or that discovery or this fact finally being established does not impact for the good of people starving or ridden with disease? Human behavior is what matters and to that end, how has science contributed to the basic good which becomes less visible with each progress?

In my academic life, thankfully now in the past, I was in constant contact and disagreement with some thought scientist or scientific thinker. At the risk of being judgmental, I must say that without exception, their take on life was that they were superior to those other mere mortals who could only hypothesize, whereas, they could prove. Their motivation was, in the end, their own advancement and financial betterment. Is that a result of our educational system, our capitalistic society, our work ethic, our lack of proper philosophical background, our youth, our desire to get ahead, our need to over achieve – to be better than the other, is it our adopted human selfishness, our drive to survive, our greed?

To that I can only say that we all have an abundance of those basic reasons and we all may make our choice. Just how much of what science has published do we actually need? Why isn't it just as important to know the history and the outcome of wars being all predicated on the same set of premises: To own the mind and property of others for our own satisfaction. We have become much more efficient at killing others and destroying our bountiful planet in the meantime.

Yet, we fail to understand or care about this. Our karma is determined by all the wrong continuing acts of *samsara*. We are acting stupidly. We should advance science for good, but there is too little in it being accomplished. How many fine and good minds are being wasted on the development of weapons? Or, for that matter, on those absolutely essential chemical creams that make your face smooth and radiant for 16 hours a day and all that research in between weapons and beauty products? Even Du Pont has dropped their self-effacing, "Better Things for Better Living Through Chemistry!" At least they are being more truthful these days. One wonders what Union Carbide's latest products can do after Buphol – or the genetic engineering profitability of Monsanto?

In place of wondering and studying how the universe was formed, would it not be far more worthwhile to expend the same energy and money on where we are going? In the film, *What the Bleep Do We Know?* the title question is appropriate, but the Quantum Physics involved cannot begin to explain the importance of the very question posed.

I want to use this film as an example of what should be termed our Western Excremental Society. It is so simple in that the question in the film title has no relevance. What possible difference does it make if the basis is ignored while they go on and on and on about how we got here. That isn't what it's all about. What it is about is that whatever it is that we do know is being ineptly applied to our needs. Disclaiming this or that or this god or that God is all very poignant, but it is irrelevant. The question should be: "*What the Bleep Are We Doing with What We Know?*" I don't blame the scientists in the film for not pushing that. As with all good scientists, they have been given a question and they try to oblige with some nice new theories on vibrations. I do, however, blame those who made up the theme for the film for being as one dimensional as the very question they ask. In their own film interviews with themselves (!) they take on such an epidermal attitude toward what could be something of value, but it never gets any further than the box office revenue. They fail to reveal their real minds, which I'm fairly certain they do possess. They haven't even scratched the peeling on the "...*Doing Here?*" question and are content with their success in making a terribly flimsy film that, "Couldn't be made because there is no demand for it," and other drivel about how they have opened an entirely new field and watch our new one we're, "releasing in early 2006."

And, the poor actress, Amanda, the talented deaf girl who plays the lead. What a victim of the filmmakers she appears to be. She has become so involved in the desperate circle of self-praise she herself thinks it's great! In their proclamations the writers and scientists involved in the construct of the screenplay minimally probe Quantum Physics and Mechanics with huge displays of special effects, but provide few answers to their own questions cleverly posed in their laboratories and libraries. They have been so immersed in the tripe of the hype they lose their credibility. They explain sight and sound and how they are interpreted. A deaf girl begins to see that her actions and attitude of self-worth acts with natural forces of the universe to create internal and external change. This is all for the good, of course.

So, what about a blind person? How would they perceive and understand in the same set of circumstances as Amanda? In the film they state that unless you have experienced something through sight you cannot perceive it in reality. That cannot be entirely correct as blind people have demonstrated their ability to play golf, hit a softball, shoot pool and hundreds of other complex activities. I don't understand such sightless producers. They would appear to be lacking in their own perceptions.

The public tends to jump before looking and that would appear to be the case of those who viewed *What the Bleep* only once or twice. So popular had the film become that the seemingly inevitable occurs in terms of market capitalization. We have the second Quest for Global Healing Conference in Bali where it was possible to "witness the richness of Balinese culture and traditions." If you did that one you were to return home with a new passion for service. In a word: Pathetic. There should be no real need to travel that far to learn so little. Everything these "World Renown Speakers," including Desmond Tutu and Walter Cronkite, can give you for their huge fees is their warmed over or newly discovered truths as revealed centuries ago by any number of Buddhist teachers. They will be exploring the potential for transformative action! How can these people ever atone for such gross commercial fraud?

You can also buy copies of *The Bleeping Herald* to learn how to trust "the voice within" and contemplation's on the String Theory and Dimensions of Thought. Or, better yet, you can buy their new book by the authors of the film and thereby discover the possibilities for altering your everyday reality.

Or, you could otherwise spend your time thinking about the Buddhist teachings, as Soygal Rinpoche has repeatedly said, "You can spend a lot of money on it or you can do it yourself free!"

The producers, director and screenwriter for *What the Bleep – Down the Rabbit Hole* are also offering an exploration into the beyond with Dean Radin, "Click here for the FREE three minute teleseminar highlight." You are also invited to join the Shift in Action program of the Noetic Sciences and once you have become a Shift in Action Partner you can actually, really and truly, gain access to the full teleseminar!

There are Bleep Groups everywhere and a Bleep Group Coordinator in Wisconsin. You can buy your Bleep in German and Betsy Chasse can introduce you to Deepak Chopra to unlock the hidden dimensions in your life while Betsy herself explains her traumatic journey from self admitted: "shoe consciousness" to even higher spirituality. And, do not think you must go naked in your own transformation because you can now buy Bleep Gear in 12 countries using your priceless cards.

75 years ago this was Flash Gordon and Buck Rogers of the Twentieth Century. Ellen De Generise waxes eloquent about "What The Bleep?" calling the movie "bleepin' great!" and actress Drew Barrymore 'rolls out of bed like a burrito' and creates her day BLEEP style. How much more intellectual power do we need than that derived from such persons to convince us that there is this new world of love and understanding out there, all of it made easy by a continuously inane Hollywood.

I cannot hold out much hope for the public or the movie makers if that is all there is. At one period in my life I did feel there was a chance that there would be a sequence of events to wake up the world to the fact that they needn't be lost in the never ending pursuit of material happiness and satisfaction. I no longer think that is possible and can only hope that some people can and will accept the fact that they must think their way out of their own dilemmas of life created for them on this planet by deceitful charlatans in constant pursuit of fame and money.

Alas, they seem convinced that happiness is their 15 minutes of fame as proclaimed by a forgettable individual of little talent.

It is discouraging, with the scientist and film makers congratulating themselves on their miniscule achievement and popularity while plotting even more and greater money making events. P.T. Barnum said over a century ago that, "There is a sucker born every minute," and that hasn't changed except the birth figures are probably higher. He needn't have noticed it from his own circus attractions because it was already there in the tent shows of the evangelists. The public has lined up to buy any form of sanctity and that is equally distressing. Instant salvation; instant intellect; it is all the same.

And, those dilemmas are yet even more thoroughly examined and the quotes from the great thinkers of the day do little more than further cloud the issues in question. We can get more quotes and more confusion about the basic causes of our social and personal distress in five minutes than the ancient philosophers could provide in a lifetime. The blame for the misinformation goes to the television, the movies, the corruption in politics, the homosexuality, and sexual freedom; it's the parents, it's because 60% of the people have drifted away from God, it's the Arabs, it's the global warming and its the pollution.

Actually, it's because we quit having to think for ourselves. No one wants anything other than simple solutions to complex problems under complex conditions. It is the field and the field is thinking and it is pretty certainly established that if you don't do your own thinking, someone else will happily do it for you. That isn't free.

Thinkers can change the world and it only takes a few thinkers who become true teachers to effect the changes. It is the exposure of ignorance and it can be a healing factor. Socrates said, "Physician, heal thyself!" He also said "Know yourself and you will know the universe and the gods." It still makes sense. It seems to me that those statements made by one of the truly great thinkers sets the parameters for everything we need to know and since he said that, things have continued to go down hill intellectually.

EPISODE 11:

BUDDHISM:
LATE MOTHER TO ALL

IN THINKING ABOUT what Socrates said, I am once again driven to establish a parallel with Buddha's teachings. Socrates very likely had never heard of Buddha, but they both could have been from the same era or school of philosophy. Given that one was East and one was West and you know the rest. Somehow, those fantastically gifted thinkers of any period or age always seem to come up with the same answers and it amazes me that later lights haven't seemed to have been content to pursue their predecessors' remarkably accurate guidelines. They do, for some reason, insist on developing their own genre, if that is the correct term for what I'm trying to think.

Buddha said the void of the universe is to be called Primordial Awareness. What that means is that by its very nature it possesses both life and intelligence. It is that which the Quantum Physicists would say is also consciousness and that consciousness is the basis for all concepts of matter and life. Perhaps, but only perhaps, that is the basis of attaining enlightenment.

Thich Nhat Hanh, the Vietnamese master, described Buddha's enlightenment in this manner:

"Guatama felt as though a prison which confined him for thousands of lifetimes had broken open. Ignorance had been the jail keeper. Because of ignorance, his mind had been obscured, just like the moon and the stars hidden by storm clouds. Clouded by endless waves of deluded thoughts, the mind had falsely divided reality into subject and object, self and others, existence and nonexistence, birth and death, and from those discriminations arose wrong views – the prisons of feelings, craving, grasping, and becoming. The suffering of birth, old age, sickness, and death only made the prison walls thicker. The only thing to do was to seize the jail keeper and see his true face. The jail keeper was ignorance… once the jail keeper was gone, the jail would disappear and never be rebuilt again."

This would be the obscuration of dualism.

It is also said that at the moment Buddha had thus conquered all the dark forces of delusion and he was rewarded for his age long patience, discipline and flawless concentration by achieving his final goal of human existence. The earth itself shuddered; no one anywhere was angry, ill or sad; no one did evil, none was proud, the world became quite quiet, as though it had reached full perfection.

What Buddha had observed was that ignorance of our true nature is our greatest failure and that ignorance is our

mind's tendency to wander in distraction. We don't concentrate. To end this constant distraction one must bring
the mind home through meditation. It is the greatest gift
one can give one's self.

Logically, this is also the greatest truth and that has to
be the most important part of our life and mental make-up.
If we believe that, and we should, there is hope for human
happiness. If our science pursues the goal of truth, then it
will not be wasted. There is good science, but to be great
science it must be directed toward the same set of values
based on the truths which Buddha clearly saw and enunciated 2,500 years ago.

In the film, *What The Bleep Do We Know,* there is a scene
where Amanda misses her train, but sees an exhibition by a
Japanese psychologist on water. He clearly proves, through
a series of pictures, that human thought can positively or
negatively influence water's molecular structure in remarkable ways. A fellow viewer remarks to Amanda that since
90 percent of our body consists of water, we should con-
sider what our thoughts can do to us. It is a very revealing
statement, later on, when Amanda declares that she hates
her body.

The movie was not made until 2005. Buddha's teachings
tell us not to think negatively about ourselves or others.

Since the 1970's the thought that one must love oneself
before others can love us has passed through our popular
psychology. The western world started catching up, but had
we had Buddha's thoughts on that subject all along there is
no reason not to believe that a hundred million lives could
have been saved by wars avoided. So, too, could the ago-
nizing question of "Who Am I?" could be replaced with

"What Am I?" for the vastly greater good of humanity. Why science cannot accept such basic philosophy is most puzzling to me. Much of science is so thoroughly wasted when it need not be... and not all science is wasted. Only excremental science, not experiential science is wasted.

With the newly developed fascination of the public with Quantum Physics it is interesting to ponder how long it will take for science to uncover what Buddha has already revealed. Science is concerned, it seems, more with how things come about than in dealing with the evident truth. While Deepak Chopra is certainly correct in saying, "Quantum discoveries enable us to go into our very atoms and remember the early universe itself," that is merely a statement of opportunity. While those in the laboratories are testing this subjectively and experientially, philosopher Roderic Knowles summarily states, "The supremacy of science as the most advanced authoritative and conclusive means of acquiring knowledge about the nature of Life, even at the purely material level, is an illusion which needs to be shattered – particularly when such a supremacy does not even exist within what it regards as its own domain."

To make the point clear, he tells of the finding of Peter Tompkin's work in his book, *The Secret Life of Nature* in which he relates the astounding discoveries of theosophists Anne Besant and Charles Leadbetter in 1908. These two extraordinary minds, using thousands of years old yogi techniques, accurately, "depicted the number of protons and neutrons in the nuclei of both arsenic and aluminum" a quarter of a century before the physicist James Chadwick actually discovered the neutron. Besant and Leadbetter, in their publication, 'Occult Chemistry,' had also described particles even smaller than the quarks, some 70 years before physicists postulated their existence. In examining the theosophist's atoms, all were found to be 100 percent accurate and later, E. Lester Smith, Fellow of the Royal Society, supported the accuracy in his work, *Occult Chemistry ReEvaluated.*

Stunningly, Knowles adds that physicists "needed one electron volt of energy to study an atom and they needed ten million electron volts to reveal a quark while Besant and Leadbetter needed none whatsoever." They even anticipated string theories.

How did Besant and Leadbetter do it? They used the technique described by 3rd century BCE Indian sage, Patanjali. His *Yoga Sutras* describes how to, "obtain knowledge of the small, the hidden or the distant by directing the light of the super physical faculty." This is within the process of enlightenment attained by Buddha.

So why don't we make use of this? Would it not, again, to use Soygal Rinpoche's terms, "be a lot less expensive" than science as currently being funded? Is it accurate? It was accurate enough for Einstein to help him cope with the magnitude and incredible depth of energy. Madam Blavatsky used her understanding of *siddhi* to underscore her vision. Science, in general, however, to maintain its position of power, not unlike the church, employs an ancient practice as well. It is the one of ignorance that Buddha has said must be vanquished and to do so the simplest, most direct and effective means is constantly in use. Again, it is what Harvard's Robert Torbert expanded from Jung and Merleau-Ponty and describes as the Mystery-Mastery Complex.

With corporate and applied science, it works this way. You assemble a body of knowledge and you keep it hidden from the public. It gives you power and enables pervasive greed to enrich. Every now and then you package it for huge profit, continuing to claim recovery of laboratory cost for decades.

As Knowles asks, "How can there ever be an all embracing 'unified theory' or 'theory of everything,' the Holy Grail of the scientific quest, if basics in the nature and dynamics of life such as thought and consciousness are constantly excluded?"

Perhaps there will be a time when the world, or at least the materialistic western world, will come to realize and accept that 'matter is derived from mind and not mind from matter' as is stated in *The Tibetan Book of the Great Liberation.* Progress and its worth must be viewed in terms of environmental and human cost.

Considering the human condition in the western world, it is quite obvious that what has been taught is largely pap. We have come to this state of spiritual ignorance through our own weakness and greed. We have a problem with being poor in possessions and in our consuming quest to overcome this undesirable state we have ignored our inner self. We all want to be as comfortable as is possible and there's nothing wrong with that if we can also include our conscience: that there is something within us that acts as our moral gyroscope. We can call it whatever we wish, but to those who have found it and understood it, it is the buddha nature we were born with if we're at all "normal" in our mental health.

No one has yet come up with an understandable description of soul excepting what the Christian church has put forth. A lot of that has to do with the idea of faith, which at times seems to be an all inclusive term which means you must believe in us as the power and not question it. In the wrong hands it can be terribly assertive and damaging. The most powerful inclusion in the paradigm of salvation is the soul. It is also the most comforting assurance of deliverance. This soul will follow your wishes. In order to get into the Kingdom of Heaven, you can repent your sins, save your soul and be at peace in the certain knowledge that no matter what you've done or how you have lived your life if you confess and repent, you get a new start and are home and dry. There is no explanation given of how your personal trespassing forgiveness affects those you have damaged. They are on their own. No one knows where this came from, but there are indications in Christian literature.

Both wisdoms of Buddhism and Hinduism share the doctrine of *samsara*. When one uses the word "doctrine," one can rightfully assume that it is firm and established. Hence it is established that *samsara* indicates that all beings pass through the unceasing cycle of birth, death and rebirth. Buddhism separates from Hindu belief of a changeless soul and an ultimate predestined identity. Humans, like all other phenomenon, change constantly and are in flux. What this means is that there is no fixed entity called "the soul." It doesn't exist and instead there is the *anaman* or non–self and this teaching rejects an unchanging core within each person. (To me, it seems there is an element of self forgiveness, though, and this is a bit perplexing in relation to ego denial.)

This being so, what is a human being and what does he/

she consist of in relative terms? First, there is the physical body made up of the four elements; earth, water, fire and air. Second are our feelings in the form of sight, smell, touch, taste, sound, thought and perceptions. These attach the categories of good, neutral or evil to our sensory inputs, habitual mental dispositions, which in turn, connect *karma* producing will to our mental activities. Finally there is consciousness, which comes to us when the mind and body come together in contact with our external world.

Spirituality, then, has no material bonding of which to become a part and one's mortality becomes apparent in its true nothingness. This brings up the obvious question of how one can improve in the next incarnation, assuming you do believe in this part of the eternal process. If there is no soul to which the good deeds can be attached, what is the meritorious grounding? The answer given is that *karma* continues in the mental energy, *samskara*, which is within one's consciousness, which, in truth, is the only thing which does survive after death of the body and this can go forward.

During life, one's goal is to continually become a better person; Good or bad acts form the *karma* consequences and the Buddhist philosophy makes it clear that *karma* is not fatalistic. It can and does change as does all phenomenon and so one's destiny is not predestined. You become better; it becomes better.

There is a connection between the philosophical doctrinal premise and Quantum Physics. It becomes more obvious as we grow to understand the scientific law that the mind can and does change a physical condition in what is thought of in the West as matter. It would seem, therefore, that the goal of meritorious rebirth has now been proven, by science, and only a mere 2,500 years after it was known to the great thinkers of Buddha's time.

While I may not yet have been convinced or convinced myself about rebirth, there is no doubt in my mind that the *samsara* system – good and bad resulting in your ultimate destiny – is a primary law for life. Trying to be a better person makes good sense.

EPISODE 12:

NATURE AS GOD

IN ATTEMPTING TO BRING the concept of man and God to-gether I have had to cope with hundreds of conflicting, or at least contrasting, beliefs. In some areas and in some respects, I have managed to come to grips with that vastness. One of my conclusions is that time and power have corrupted the true image of man's universal God. The Christian church, over the centuries, has separated God from the people. In the Buddhist belief, it is held that I Am God, and so there is no revered God or outside god entity. The latter seems to me to be in a better intellectual position. The ancient communion of man and nature represented the nearness of God with man's conscience. Irish history has no creation stories; the earth and we have always been here and there is no record of a deity intervening with nature or existing independent of it. In pre-Christian Ireland there was the concept of *neart*; the power or force that animated the world.

In reading Chet Raymos' book, *Climbing Brandon*, he talks about the time in Irish Christian history that it was believed all nature was holy. Ireland's own Augustinus Hibernicus wrote in 655 AD that the miracles of the Scriptures must be interpreted within the context of nature's laws, not in contravention of them... the vision of nature as a harmonious whole, whose integrity not even God will violate. Nature as God, infinite as the field, can be just as mystifying in the abyss of its depth. Was Augustinus knowingly echoing Buddha when he wrote in *The Miracles of the Holy Scripture* that "whoever desires true wisdom make haste to the eternal kingdom where there is no ignorance?" Was his eternal kingdom the enlightenment Buddha sought and discovered 2,500 years before Augustinus?

On page 36 of his book, Raymos talks of the God of orthodox Christianity entering the world in the guise of his desexualized Son, the offspring of a virgin, and then only temporarily. His message is clear: "The world of nature is a base and fallen place to be abandoned as soon as possible for the transcendent and immaterial advantages of heaven."

Raymos quotes John Carey, who teaches Early and Medieval Irish at the National University of Ireland in Cork, "Existence itself, then, is the ultimate miracle; had our eyes not grown so dull, they would be dazzled with the ineffable wonder wherever we turned our gaze."

Those eyes were dulled by the same doom and gloom of modern Christianity that provokes, not thought, but dulling fear. Buddha has said we are God. With knowing nature, we understand ourselves, hence we understand the existence of the buddha within. The greed which developed in the church devoured the edacious divinity of their priests and God's place was allowed to be usurped by human interpretation. In pre Roman Catholic times, nature taught man to be pious and respectful, prayerful and understanding.

The loci shifted with the dominance of the church and man now resorts to a second power to get to the object of their theology; an everlasting life. So distorted has it become that man can no longer accept life on this planet as being the center of purpose, but rather a church directed and taught ethereal after-being. Prayers are directed to God in their language of a dogma established by biblical consensus and with their narrow protocol.

This centralization of power and the dominant will to interpret what was sworn to be the word of God has done wondrous things for organized religion, but the corruption that has inevitably followed has done more to ruin the decency of mankind than any other organization in all of history. I am reminded of Voltaire who waged a twenty five year war upon this intolerance through his writing and his deeds. Voltaire was not an atheistic; he accepted the few and brief tenets of "natural religion"… a belief in a transcendent Deity and obedience to the moral precepts that God had revealed to man through his reason. What he attacked were the particular dogmas, the accretions of theology, the complex mysteries and contradictory ceremonials of Christianity that through the ages has engendered fanaticism, persecution and bloodshed, suppressed reason and persecuted free thought. Things have hardly improved in the 230 plus years since Voltaire's death, which should give us some clue as to the aforementioned power and will of religious leaders.

The primacy of Buddhist acceptance of the *samsaric* human condition could hardly be more different, and yet it is the same as ancient western beliefs. In Buddhism there is the understanding that, again, there is a buddha within us all. What could be more natural, then, than to direct one's meditations toward ourselves and the rest of humanity to be lifted to a better, more perfect life on earth? The enveloping condition of conscience is enlarged to include all sentient beings. Early, pre Roman Christian monks must have experienced the same oneness with nature, self and God in the darkness of their cells and beehive hut existence. How can we question that one is different than the other: That the promise of everlasting life through prayer is any more or less fulfilling than the silent Buddhist, enwrapped in contemplative conscience and without wonder who they are or where they are going.

And yet, in our western lives, there is so much fuss and bother about being saved. There seems to be a psychotic condition connected to being a Christian in good standing. It is becoming obvious to me that the power of the organized church has destroyed far more by denial than it has positively redeemed. The established rules are explicit, but who wrote them? Who made them up and codified them? Who established the boundaries of such rigid constancy? The same hierarchy of Jews and Christian mortals who would have the gall and the audacity to write off Mohammed as an exotic mushroom eating, uneducated Arab who happened to marry Fatima, a camel rich widow 600 years too late.

There is none of that self-righteous judgment in my Buddhist beliefs, yet from my own Judeo-Christian heritage I, too, make the same judgments of Christianity so my *samsaric* fate is conditioned by my dualistic background. We Western people have that spiritual history in as much as we have been conditioned by the church to accept superior wisdom as the church chooses to interpret it. They epitomize the Mystery-Mastery Concept over and over and over again. It is, "I Know, You Don't." To me that is a sad, pathetic premise upon which to base your spiritual life.

The benefits of Christian charity are many and great, but in some cases it is predicated on acceptance of their faith. I think of the Famine Days in Ireland when the starving only got the soup when they discarded the "O' " from their Catholic names and became simply a nice Protestant Boyle or Mahony or whatever. There was such a price to stay minimally alive, comparable to some Catholics to selling their souls to the Devil. Many died because they wouldn't trade their "faith" for a cup of gruel just to stay alive one more tortured day. They died as heathens would. That's not God's way. That may be some god's way, but not God's way as a Christian should see it.

All of this is not to say that fear does not exist or isn't traded upon in Buddhism where *The Six Realms of Being* exists. As I understand things personally, until the human being realizes *nirvana* they are destined to be reborn and undergo "re-death" as a result of having acted out of ignorance and greed. So, here, too, one sees that you better get yourself straight or you will not just go to a hell, you will continue to go there until you banish ignorance in your earthly lifetimes.

Speaking of hell, I'm having a bad time with my Western mind-fix in dealing with these concepts, but the more I see of them, the more they do impart a sense of a meaningful purpose to ridding oneself of the *samsara* cycle. Commonly, the *samsara* recognizes *The Six Realms of Being* and you are reborn according to how well you have behaved and it seems to go like this:

Realm One: Since only humans enter *nirvana* , this is an existential state, so do not waste the privilege of human birth and the opportunity to live the teachings of Buddha (Dharma).

Realm Two: Having had a good purpose in human life you may be reborn in a heavenly state (deity). Living there you enjoy all the same advantages of earthly existence, but there are also those advantages provide the temptation of attachment which can and which will impede you in your spiritual practice. It is still the best place to be and is attainable through devotion. You are on probation or you are in a minor Catholic condition of Purgatory… or so it seems to me.

Realm Three: Reborn here, you have power, but it is demonically predicated and dominated by anger. These a*shura* (demons) can be very troublesome and bring humans illness and unhappiness.

Realm Four: This is to be reborn as a restless spirit and only bodies of "subtle matter." This is truly a terrible state to be in and features invisible figures, born with big stomachs and little throats. Compassionate Buddhists in better States of Being don't fear them, but they do feed them.

Realm Five: This would be the Buddhist equivalent of hell or the real Purgatory, with eight hot cells and eight cold cells. You have produced some very bad *karma* to end up here where you could be eaten alive. You got here by lying, cheating, theft or adultery. Buddhist teachers of the young and old alike use this threat of Realm Five to inspire good moral behavior.

I think I know where I am going, but I will be in the company of friends.

Realm Six is to be reborn into the animal world and exhibit but a few indications of having a conscience. It is exemplified by the preying on one another and this is to be avoided. Getting out of here must take a great deal of doing.

Then there is the horrible Tibetan Wheel of Life, which is a map of *samsara* and uses three animals to symbolize the *Klesha,* or poisons that cause the generation of really bad *karma*. First is the pig for delusion; second the rooster for lust and third is the snake for anger and hatred. There is also the ugly demon, *Yama,* which encloses the Wheel of Life and he is the Lord of Death. He represents the human tendency to cling to material existence. Unfortunately, Yama is believed to oversee the karmic retribution

So, all of that is scary and terribly pessimistic. I would have to doubt you could teach that in the public schools. But it does point out to me that the Western mind is so intent on material gain that it would be hard to bring the understanding of many people to Buddhism based on these horrible fears and restrictions. Buddhists do say that it is okay to be rich, but unless you had your riches dropped upon you from heavenly sources, you don't stand much of a chance in the world of business to get to the riches and still stay out of Realms Three through Six!

It may be comfortable enough to endorse and practice the Buddhist teachings, or Dharma, but at the same time it is very difficult to live in the ancient life style under the conditions of *The Six Realms of Being* as a future outlook for your other lives. I can't have those lives hanging over my head, but if they are there; if I were to really believe the whole of the Dharma as a guideline, I simply cannot make it. I can only live my life as best I can. Just as some great painters painted in "the school of Rembrandt" or Titian, or Tinterreto, or whoever, I can live my life in the school of Buddha, but not as a genuine Buddhist can or does live. I can have the buddha within to guide me, but I cannot hope to follow his moral path to *nirvana*.

There is no way I can deny the path toward a better life. It is the same path Buddha prescribed for reaching *nirvana*. These are the *Four Noble Truths* and the first of these he identifies is that of suffering. These are the inevitable mortal experiences of mental and physical sickness, the loss of loved ones, our own old age and then our death. It teaches us that even pleasure, at some point, ends, but rather than teaching pessimism, it is meant to make us clearly aware of our human conditions.

With the *First Noble Truth* of suffering we realize that birth is suffering, old age is suffering, sickness is suffering, death is suffering, sorrow and lamentation, grief, pain and despair are suffering, disassociation from the pleasant is suffering and not to get what we want is suffering. In brief, the five aggregates (*skandhas*) of attachment are suffering.

Understanding this also allows us to understand that everyone has the same inevitable ending. Seeing suffering in others should mean that we should show compassion and loving kindness to all mankind. The escape from *samsara* is through the spiritual means of seeking liberation from it.

A refuge is found in the Dharma and the community of the sangha.

The Second Noble Truth is that the cause of suffering is desire in excess of biological need. It is so pervasive that it shaped the evolution of the earth. The first beings of our planet were non material, leading blissful lives. Then one of them tasted the sweet substance covering the earth and became addicted to it. Others followed and their radiance disappeared; they soon had solid bodies, then divided themselves by unlike tastes, then discovered sex and the rest is history. I cannot help but wonder about this Pali text and the later story of God creating Adam from the clay of the earth; the story of temptation and eating the apple. Again, the Pali story precedes the Genesis, just as Noah's ark followed the Babylonian story of the Flood.

The answer to solving the problems created by the *Second Noble Truth* is that the body must sustain life, but the Buddha must practice the art of equanimity.

Scientists are now able to distinguish between lust and lasting attachment. They tell us that love and obsessive-compulsion disorder could have a similar chemical profile, therefore love and mental illness could be difficult to tell apart. They want to rid the equation of Freud and the oedipal transcendent complex. Typically, the scientist wishes to reduce everything to the simplest form and obviate the puzzling questions given rise by human emotion. It is just a percentage figure of testosterone in the male bloodstream, and sooner or later the fuel runs low and passion exits from the romantic bond.

When love lasts it is called commitment, and that commitment is founded on selflessness and devotion to your partner's happiness and contentment. If this is a chemical element it would be proper to leave it alone and not try to make more of it. To define it further or to analyze its content has no value... and one does not always know the difference between desire and commitment at the crucial time of decision making.

The scientists have so far been unable or unwilling to take on the other side of the equation involving the female instinct for motherhood. We could reduce the human equation down to basic human failure by saying we have testosterone in the nomadic male on one side and the female instincts and desire to procreate on the other. The result seems to be babies being born whose fathers have disappeared to go hunting again.

This is not equanimity, but it does illustrate the intensity of human problems while attempting to walk the line. Soygal Rinpoche encompasses more than the *Second Noble Truth*, but gives balance to it all by saying:

> We are what we think
> Hate has never dispelled hate,
> only love dispels hate.
> Speak or act with an impure mind
> and trouble will follow you.
> All that we are arises
> from our thoughts
> Speak or act with a pure mind
> and happiness will follow you
> like a shadow, unshakable

The Third Noble Truth is that removing desire removes suffering. The cyclical law of *samsara* can be ended through the constant application of the quotation above. The *Nirvana* or enlightenment can only come through the cultivation of the insight most often accomplished through meditation. Enlightenment can be achieved, but I believe it is probably the most uncommon event in human history. It is far, far more difficult than simple Christian redemption and that's likely why heaven is so crowded with happy souls and why no one can even begin to describe *nirvana*; the closest description being the moment of entry into the enlightened condition.

The Fourth Noble Truth leading to the cessation of suffering is *The Noble Eightfold Path*. It is a very practical goal-directed guide and Buddha illustrated the need to get on with it by his story of the man who was struck with a poison arrow. It does no good for the victim to ask who shot him, or where it hit him, or what wood the shaft was or whether it was accidental. He must remove the poison immediately or he will die, so why philosophize about it?

In his definition of *The Eightfold Path,* Buddha rejected two ideas held by world religions. First is the transcendent God and man's relationship with a creator. The second is the rejection of man possessing an immortal soul. To Buddha, this was a false consolation and like God, it is man's projection of our desire-driven mind searching for security through immortality.

At first, this seemed harsh to me, but then I do believe that *we are what we think* and that *we are what we will be*, so that's now just fine with me. I'm happy with what I'll get. I don't think I feel like a person being re-born as a Christian, because once you are reborn, I think that must give you a false sense of security and I don't have or want that security blanket. I must continue to work on it, everyday. What I can relate to is the thought I read about from Fiona Butler, the Irish Psychologist who said it's okay to have your head in the stars, but you have to have your feet on the ground. And like her, I will do my best to show compassion to all sentient beings and she said, "It doesn't always work, but I do try!"

The Eightfold Path can be said to consist of three parts. The *first* is morality, which is made up of right speech, right action and right livelihood. The *second* category is meditation, which is right mindfulness and right concentration and the *third* is development of wisdom or insight through taking the right view and thinking the right thoughts. I don't think Buddha ever said it would be easy and I am thinking to myself, what a much more difficult path it is nowadays with the addition of technology bringing a thousand more opportunities for me to get involved with at least a half a dozen *kleshas* per hour on a daily basis. There is a mighty temptation to call out for help, "Lord, deliver me!" but then I remember, He isn't taking my calls.

The Eightfold Path does remind me of yet another anomaly and that is the Ten Commandments given the Jews by Moses. Moses, if I got this right, came down from the mountain with them. He had gotten them from God – carved in stone as the pictures in the Bible show.

Buddha got the *Four Noble Truths* and the *Noble Eightfold Path* by meditating until he became enlightened. Did God speak to Buddha as he did to Noah? Apparently not that God because there was already the god within Buddha. He was already God as are all of us when we listen.

It is said there are several steps or stages on the path to

nirvana and the first is called, "the stream enterers." They already have the belief necessary and realize the self to be illusory. Those so dedicated will have no more than seven rebirths before attaining *nirvana*. At a more advanced stage the believer will be a "once reborn," meaning they are but one rebirth away from the goal of *nirvana*. Realizing *nirvana* is as far as most will ever make it. After that there could be the next Buddha, Maitreya, who is yet to come.

In Judaism this would be the Messiah. In Christianity we already have Jesus the Christ. The earliest story is that of Buddha, so I am again left to wonder if everything in the religions of the world isn't just attempts to re-write Buddhist teachings to meet their own needs and desires for power and glorification. But then, I have already agreed that there is nothing new and so I could conclude that Buddhism is a development.

With that thought it makes it even harder for me to not be judgmental, again going against what I am striving for and against being compassionate toward all sentient beings.

EPISODE 13:

MORAL PROGRESS AS THE FOUNDATION

THERE IS SO MUCH TO LEARN, so much to do. I am in the state of realization that there is not much time in which to review and revisit the Dharma and it has awakened me to make yet another comparison on the condition of morality.

I am such a poor Christian candidate, and yet I know that if I was to embrace it and study it as I have Buddhism over the past five years I'd be miles ahead. I keep running into myself on the tenets of the Christian path to salvation. I know I shouldn't have that problem, but that's the problem in itself. It's just too easy to go to confession and to be forgiven or to proclaim my love of Jesus just to get myself off the hook. And, there's a very good reason for this continual gnawing at my conscience and guilt determination.

I was taught a very long time ago that you should never

say you're sorry unless you really mean it. That has stuck with me and at the times when my lips have said I'm sorry and my heart and mind know that isn't really true. I feel absolutely terrible because that's so horribly wrong and immoral of me. That's why I can't accept confession or make a proclamation as a truly heartfelt cleansing, because I know very well that once I've been forgiven I'll have the tendency to repeat my misdeeds, perhaps even feeling I've gotten away with something for the moment. I simply cannot any longer accept that another mere human, acting with self-created God-given power, can say it's okay. The whole thing is full of holes if I don't place my "faith", which I cannot, in the very institution which I feel has misconstrued and has powered its way to a position of enormous influence, which to me is unbelievable. I cannot go along with just accepting that because they say they are acting in the name of God that they are!

This attitude places yet another mess on my plate. Some of the finest men and women I know have accepted the role of priest or minister; all acting on God's Word. There is not one shred of doubt in my mind that there is an overwhelming percentage of them that are convinced that they are speaking and writing with God's will in their own hearts and minds. They have dedicated their lives to the betterment, solace and the understanding of others. Many are intelligent, warm hearted and humble. The part I fail to understand is what led them to become believers and to later become the interpreters they are expected to be.

Yet, they do believe and they do continue to submit to the authority of the organization they represent without questioning what part is God's will and what part is the command of those who are acting as the directors. There have been fewer and fewer priests ordained and fewer and fewer nuns who wear the cloth or accept the order. The majority of the reasons given for this would seem to be that it is just too difficult – too demanding. A sub-cause given is the celibacy at issue and no one can argue that hormones often control our actions far more persuasively than our minds. For the nuns, there are fewer and fewer parochial schools asking for them, primarily because of the Catch 22: there are none to answer the call. They would love to have them, but they just aren't there in the numbers they once had. The disrespectful and even dangerous treatment they are subjected to by some of today's students is undoubtedly a very strong negative factor.

On the other hand, there are more Protestant ministers being graduated each year to meet the demands of a population growth and the popularity of being born again. There are a couple of obvious reasons for the imbalance for me to wonder about there, too. Becoming a priest is a far more difficult achievement, both academically and in terms of time required than the standards set in some Bible colleges. Perhaps there are reasons within the academic regime that gives pause to would-be priests as well as the ministerial student. Perhaps there are those who start to doubt it just as much as I do, and that's why they drop out or just fail to even start in the profession.

The point I'm making for myself has once again come back to hit me head on. That's the part of being judgmental. It's fine for me to judge myself, but I wonder what my personally selected guru, Padmasambhava would say about it. What I see in his teachings, certainly alongside all the others, is overwhelming compassion for all six classes of sentient beings and so I have my answer in quite a straight-forward manner: Stop being judgmental and start being compassionate. In that the teachers warn of our weakness of ego and what we would call, perhaps, a state of self satis-faction and smugness.

If I stay with Padmasambhava for very long I become confused and overwhelmed by the mind and knowledge of the man and I must pardon myself and sneak away into a corner to reflect on my ignorance. When I regain some form of control I can move to his and other teacher's inter-preters who can tell me about the deeper meanings of the morality I have sought to learn.

One of those erudite commentators of Buddhist teach-ings lived in the 5th Century CE and wrote, *"Paths of Purity."* His name was Buddhagshosa and he called mo-rality and meditation the two legs of Buddhism on which liberating insight stands. Without the moral progress there is no foundation for successful meditation. There are plenty of explanations of what is moral and what isn't and whether the immoral act was intentional or imposed, but what the oldest teachings in Therevadan belief seems to be summarized by five precepts: No intentional taking of life; no stealing; no sexual misconduct; no lying and no intoxication.

At my age, three out of five are easy for me, but the first and fourth could still present a problem. Buddhist morality is predicated on action, speech and livelihood so if you are taking the right action, you don't kill, steal or harm others and you must eat the right foods; primarily vegetarian.

Right speech means just that. Silence is better than

speaking and since we are what we think, I am constantly in deep, deep contravention. A bad speech act can lead to a lot of suffering and such thoughts fester in the mind, multiplying the damage and the danger. It's very complicated. You have to wonder how one can live with so many restrictions on what you think, say and act on.

Right livelihood is hard to cope with, too, as a measure of morality. It pretty much knocks out all westerners because you can't be a hunter, a butcher or an executioner and the last one applies to armies and other military organizations promoting violence against enemies. So, then, we can go all the way back to those Christian Crusaders again. That condemns all of us who haven't, throughout the history of mankind, been extreme pacifists.

To me, all of this brings up some difficult questions regarding those whose choice it has been to follow *The Noble Eightfold Path* to its ultimate goal; *nirvana*. What is to happen to all of those who support the monks with their begging bowls? There several levels of acceptance in the re-birth process that gives credit for those who work to support those whose vocation is ultimate enlightenment. Thus the compassion we are to find and use is exercised in the karmic rebirth of those poor lay people. As there is no creator or God, is everyone condemned to the agonies of *samsara* for eternity just as are the souls of the non-Christians who have never embraced Jesus as the Christ or who simply never heard of Jesus or his teachings? The cyclical nature of all religious questions is, perhaps, the greatest possible truth to human meaning.

Yet, my meditation seems to become easier, virtually each day and it does involve the essentials of right effort, right mindfulness and concentration. For the one long period when I was diverted into trance-like states, I did learn a good deal about two forms of mental discipline and I'm going back there as soon as I get to the natural state of mindfulness in my practice.

It is very good to be able to practice and to bring the mind home, but to advance along *The Noble Eightfold Path* I am at a huge disadvantage as are most westerners. You must have an experienced mentor to do this, to gain insight, to develop mental clarity and free oneself from negativity. Since right concentration involves trance meditation I must erase those pre-conditions which I developed so unconsciously before. My trance-like state was certainly from some scuba of learned subjective concentration, and it did lead to the "one pointedness" Buddha has elucidated. I was not ever, however, able to produce or was I ever given the condition whereby I devolved from the duality of self and other. This is but one area in which a teacher would be essential to my meditative progress.

Most certainly I have never been able to achieve the insight meditation which focuses the mind on the ultimate clarity about the very essence or nature of reality. Far from it, I am still at a great distance from the comprehensive states of my own mortality, from whatever my suffering is or will be and the critical state of accepting non-self. I could stay light years away from the non-self of being without a soul and still be searching for the insight to help rid myself of the permanence of ignorance which I feel and know I am entrapped. Without a teacher here in the west in whom I can place my complete trust it is doubtful that my meditation will ever slow down my "experience of experience" to achieve anything near the means of liberation. I will continue to struggle mightily to understand the difference between my non-soul existence and my conscience as I think I live it. Like the begging monks with the bowls, I am out there somewhere. Is it enough just to do one's best to follow the guidelines down *The Noble Eightfold Path* to becoming a decent person even if not getting within a zillion miles of *nirvana*? I think so.

If so, then stumbling down *The Noble Eightfold Path,* while never, ever even reaching the suburbs of *nirvana,* at least gives me an experience with *The Four Noble Truths.* The right view and the right thought will eventually mean an active detachment from cruelty and hatred and I think I am well on my way with that and the measure of that is *prajma*, or wisdom. That wisdom enables us to look at and see reality without anger or hatred and without greed and without that natural bugaboo, lust. You are also able to accept death and suffering in your earthly life. I've lived through some of it and the guilt and denial, which some say are psychological, I am beginning to think have been planted there by the Judeo-Christian ethics of organized religion. Does not being judgmental also mean not to think? Where is the dividing line between being judgmental and intellectual challenge? Roderic Knowles reminds us that discrimination is vital, but without the condemnation.

One can always wish for or hope for simple answers to complex questions and that's the one thing the Christians are superior at doing. They will take care of everything for you if you have the faith. Buddhism also has a simple solution, and it is all found in that same simple phrase: You are what you think. The difference between the two is also quite simple. You have faith if you wish to be a Christian because it's all about soul and immortality. In Buddhism you are always responsible for your own future and it involves just as many rules as the Christian faith.

The rejection of the unchanging soul is within the doctrine of impermanence. There is no one within. That's you and not the self centered ego and letting go of ego certainly helps start one on the way to freedom. All that energy once used to bolster that false ego or self is freed for other purposes, i. e., getting rid of the materialistic value system the western mind has developed and cherished since time immemorial.

Just from my own practice I know that it is workable. It can be done because I also know from my own meditation that when they say it is merit producing, it really is. If the practice is practiced correctly, and there really is no "wrong way", it lessens greed and the daily grind producing anger. It produces that wonderful acceptance of reality. I'm told that with instruction our meditation, in its more advanced states, can do away with past *karmas*. It can eventually lead to such detachment that *karma* is completely cut off and one's mind can find the clarity leading to enlightenment. It is also said this can be achieved in one lifetime. I'm not up for that or anything much more than a feeling of the happiness produced by knowing I've tried to become a decent man by the time I've put my mouth to the ground; "on the hard, knotty, wet roots of this land."

There is a traditional sequence of artistic renderings done by Shubun in the 15th century which captures the Mayahan path to enlightenment that I find evocative. It depicts the world as empty. There is this no-nothingness so there is really is no-thing to which one can be attached. It is known as "Ox herding" and it compares the search for enlightenment with the herder looking for his ox. It goes like this:

1. "Seeking the Ox"; being lost in *samsara* but searching for the higher truth.
2. "Finding the Tracks"; is listening, studying the land for a trace.
3. "First Glimpse of the Ox"; Meditation serves to give the beginning of *prajna.*
4. "Catching the Ox"; Beginning to understand the drawbacks of selfhood.
5. "Taming the Ox"; Beginning to understand the bliss of one's new freedom.
6. "Riding the Ox Home"; Complete freedom.
7. "Ox Forgotten, Self Alone"; Enjoying the freedom.
8. "Both Ox and Self Forgotten"; Experiencing ultimate emptiness.
9. "Returning to the Source"; Seeing the true natural world as a sphere of innate enlightenment.
10. "Entering the Market With Helping Hands"; The bodhisattva ideal as the final vocation after enlightenment.

I cannot even begin to imagine how difficult this entire process must appear to be for any young person who is being introduced to it and for them to undertake a lifetime's work to accomplish it. And, there are no promises of salvation. It is hard work and for a western mind, absolutely daunting.

I brought up a question in my last exercise in circumlocution and the answer I gave myself was not nearly comprehensive enough. I wondered if the lay people who supported the monks could expect any rebirth compensation. I thought they would quite surely be rewarded. That only caused me to wonder how that part worked and what further questions and answers it would engender.

What existed thousands of years ago and continues forever on earth is the social contract Buddha forged when he founded his first monastic order. The Sangha, or monastic community, would draw support from the laity. Wherever the Theravadan tradition of Buddhism exists, the alms giving by the laity defines the relationship. The laity is committed to the Dharma and the Sangha by their formal recitation of *The Triple Refuge*. The recitation is repeated aloud three times and interpreted from the ancient Pali language the lines are:

"To the Buddha I go for refuge; to the Dharma I go for refuge; to the Sangha I go for refuge."

So strong is the pledge that it is also recited at many public ceremonies and is led by a monk. Those who have made the pledge and who actively give material support gain the greatest karma benefit and stand in good stead to improve their field of merit and advance through their generosity. The offering of food can be made either to the monks in their bowls or taken directly to the monastery. It varies from country to country, and in some places the offering can be made in money. *The Triple Refuge* ritual and the offerings define the person as a Buddhist. The act of generosity or giving also represents several other desired positions of the lay person. It is opening up to others; it represents the loosening of the bonds of material attachment, and it shows thought for others.

In addition to or following the recitation of *The Triple Refuge* ritual, the individual may want to take up the *Five Precepts* that are derived from *The Noble Eightfold Path*, which means they refrain from harming others, stealing, sexual misconduct, lying or intoxication. Further opportunities are available to the lay community in the form of exemplary lives according to *The Noble Eightfold Path* such as going to important temples, or holy sites, turning prayer wheels and prostrating themselves at the holy places.

It all seems related to the later Christian practices. There are the churches/temples; The Ten Commandments/*The Noble Eightfold Path;* tithing/generosity; holy sites/holy sites; collection plates/money offering; mission work/generous acts, and dozens of other similarities. The devotional element of Christians is well known and a respected necessity for the complete cycle of the religion. In Buddhism, however, since Buddha was a human being and not a god that fact should negate any idea that he can help anyone in the traditional sense of devotion or worship. There is a similarity between "going for refuge" and the devotional activities found in most religions. There seems to be a good deal of textual and archaeological evidence that there has always been a degree of devotional activity related to him despite his cautions not to do so. He didn't plan it to be done, in fact he made it quite clear that it wasn't he who could help his followers, but that only the individual could begin the process of freeing oneself from the endless cycle of *samsara*.

What I have had to conclude is that the venerating of relics and other acts are a form of natural human self piousness, but based on the generosity of Buddhist teachings. You cannot just accept that knowing the truth is enough;

his word and his image must be venerated to achieve personal satisfaction, right or wrong as it might be. Even the act of reading devotional literature or reflecting on Buddha's various deeds is a form of devotion in itself and so the whole question may well have become moot. The human creature, in its innate form, possesses the need to find a symbolic security outside the ordinary mind; outside sem.

I, therefore, confess to being baffled by the idea of pilgrimage to sacred sites. I don't really see the need to be associated with the places where Buddha visited or stayed. Yet, there is something in it from which an incredible state of happiness or satisfaction is drawn. Nor can I understand the making of oneself prostrate or circumambulation or how it ever got started. Perhaps Buddha did recommend such acts, but that doesn't make it any more understandable because to me it denigrates the person who performs in such ways. So, if we are all equal, why? I'll probably never accept it though there might be something to it. I make visits to Dzogchen Beara, but it isn't a pilgrimage; it's just a chance to learn more and to be with like-minded people. I do understand the ethics of Buddhism and the do's and don'ts, so perhaps somewhere within the human psyche there exists a corollary between the good and the apparent need for devotion being exercised through physical acts. The connection between the acts and the motivation toward selflessness, I suppose, is there in abundance.

This all connects directly with Buddha's death and his assurances to his followers that when he was gone what he had taught would live on in his place. Just as in Ireland in early Christian times when the monks preserved what was left of a Western "civilization" the monks then began to assemble the Buddha's "Dharma Body." The story is told that a convening or assembly of 500 arhats was made in a large cave at Aluvihara in Sri Lanka in the 1st Century BCE. They recited what each could remember of Buddha's sermons and those recitations were judged by the elders who then recorded the entire Tipitaka and the *Pali* commentaries. The three parts became known as the "Three Baskets" and were written on palm leaves first and later on birch bark, cloth and copper plates. Some of the 1st Century birch bark scrolls still exist, and many of the *sutras* traveled to China to become recorded as the first paper texts.

The Mahayana texts became expanded and this, to me, leads to interpretation which is one of my pet peeves, but that's what history is all about. It is certainly the most difficult of reasons why I question the Bible. How much, other than the original words of Buddha should be considered doctrinal and how much is merely literary? I am forced to again wonder how much of this practice of translation became *de rigueur,* the "innate proclivity"; the *denier ressort?* If I am to wonder about the Old Testament as being a document susceptible to human deviation or error, I must accept that the expansion of the written Dharma Body could be human wishes and not the exact doctrine set forth by Buddha's words.

That extends to the translations from the Indian Theravadan to Mahayanan, to Tibetan, to Chinese and all the way down to my own interpretation. As in all, the intention may be far better than the act. We may want or even need to believe, but how much is truly Buddha and how much belongs to 10,000 translators? I am once again at odds with the word "faith." All are but conceptualizations of the original intent and thought and convictions of the one master.

I believe it was Mark Blum who wrote that this was one of the marks of the Mahayana culture in being so critical of language, "because words inevitably mean different things to different people," and no word perfectly conveys what it intends to represent. Hence, Buddha's words, when in the written form, have lost absolute authority and even the Two Truths, "conventional truth" and "ultimate truth" are logically open philosophies. Conventional truth is measurable in fact and ultimate truth is seen as being beyond description by language. The written words of the Buddhist scripture is then in the category of conventional truth.

I think I am presently of the belief that language, or translation of thought, is too unreliable to be deemed the truth. If this is the case, then I belong with the Zen school. They have the belief that truth can only be transmitted non-verbally. And, that's the whole point. Truth is beyond mind. The Buddha was very clear about it. Paraphrasing his words, he said listen to what I say, but don't believe what I say. Test it. If it works for you, great; if it doesn't, leave it. We often fret too much about impracticalities.

Whatever I may wonder about that which underlies all the thousands of pages of translation from the extant vernacular, I am certain in the basis of morality. The straightforwardness of *The Noble Eightfold Path* might not have been from the exact, syllable for syllable word of the Buddha, but the behavior outlined or dictated is unmistakably correct. That the Buddha was rewarded with enlightenment for the perfection of his earlier lives can be believed or disbelieved, but the lesson of his absolute morality cannot be questioned by the likes of me.

What I do wonder about, still, is why I persist in making a comparison between Buddhist and the Christian beliefs or why anyone else should. It really shouldn't be a contest and there is a choice with the ultimate opinion being that both are right for us so fortunate as to be here to discuss it.

EPISODE 14:

CONCLUSION

Thoughts and Reflections

WHEN I WAS A YOUNG MAN growing up in Big Lake, Minnesota, there was not much in the way of entertainment from outside the home. Of course, there was no television, but there was the magical box of a radio and on this radio, station WCCO. Every evening there was a program with a local writer and hence, a celebrity, named Cedric Adams. Cedric was a bit of a rogue and drank far too much according to some, but if that's what it takes, pass the bottle, please. He did an occasional segment on his show and in his newspaper column in the Minneapolis Tribune called "Thoughts While Shaving" and that sort of thinking has always captured my imagination. Indulge me, please.

IF THE REBIRTH IS NOTHING MORE than the scientific fact of

genes, either good or bad, isn't *karma* the inheritance of blood quality?

Wasn't Peteonius right when he said, "Fear made the gods" and hence all the religions of mankind are made by frightened men?

The philosopher Hobbes said that religion is that which is allowed and superstition is that which isn't allowed.

J.M. Robertson wrote *PAGAN CHRISTS* and it was published by Dorset Press in New York in 1987. Mr. Robertson was born on the Isle of Aran in 1856 and died in 1933 so he was safe when that was published. The neo's would surely have made him pay for what he said in the book, but nevertheless, some of what he wrote needs to be listened to now. He said Gods and Goddesses are created out of men's needs and passions. Add to that desires and wishes because once embraced, they all become personal deities.

Once a religion has a sacred book, the *Dharma Body* in the Buddhist case, its traditions, triumphs, its established worship, then the conservatism of the religious instinct counts for more in preserving it than the measure of genius that went into making it. The progress of a religious system is primarily the result of political maneuvering.

All religions appear to be pantheistic in that they are derivative, changeable and susceptible to man's desires and the need for a supernatural power base. It represents the ethic of seeking its own ends. One can witness this if you observe the changes in how bible colleges, seminaries or even monasteries are administered. They meet the political need.

If you are going to gamble on religion, since the after

life is so huge, it may be better to enhance your odds by worshiping more than one god.

One has to think about this unless one's brain has been numbed from birth.

Science and philosophy are rational; religion fills in the irrational gaps of which there are as many as the stars in the sky.

God and the angels are somehow acceptable substitutes for polytheism and no more ridiculous.

Religion is every bit as revisionist as the later invention called "history." If the Jews had not been exiled and had not gone to Babylon their monotheism would have died.

Is it possible that the Messianic belief came as a direct result of the Jews being persecuted and enslaved?

Jesus/Joshua existed before the death of Herod, and the name "Jesus" is a variant of Joshua.

So what is all the fuss about, the talk and worry over creation and religion if it turns out that recent science proves true that our origin may have begun as a result of chemical reaction wherein cells turn received energy and accompanying atoms into biologically significant molecules? The carbon molecules involved, such as a vinegar-like acetic acid and citric from fruit have been around for about four billion years. The 11 identified molecules involved could have been the key role players in the development of biochemical; hence metabolism first before the cells, then replication, then life.

Logos is used by the Jews for The Word, but Logos came to Jerusalem from the Greeks. It is also possible that it was already there, having been adopted from... pause... the Babylonians! And since Babylon is in the identified area of earliest civilizations, it all just developed from that same fear factor.

Regardless, the Jews developed the speculation of Logos and perfected their religious laws in accordance with it. Close *pagan* parallels are virgin birth, sacrificial death and resurrection.

There just isn't enough evidence to support the gospels. Even that which is credited to the Old Testament is not truly theirs in origin. Again, it came from Babylon.

Robertson wrote about the same questions I had about the Dharma since it wasn't written down for centuries after it was first enunciated and has many divergent interpretations. It does bear resemblance to the contemporary Jainist movement with the exception of the severe austerities practiced by some of the sects.

It didn't claim to be a new teaching. Gotama (Robertson's spelling) was only one of a long series of Buddhas as there were 24 before him. After one Buddha dies his religion flourishes for a period, then decays and a new Buddha emerges to teach the lost Dharma or Truth. Any number of teachings attributed to "the Buddha" may be brought to question as the records do clash:

1. The Buddha speaks of gods he believes in.
2. He discourages sacrifices, yet he then endorses them.
3. He proclaims an egalitarian position, but keeps honoring Brahmin Arahats.
4. Much of the teachings credited to him did not come from him.
5. Much of his basic philosophy was extant before his birth.

Further, *karma* was not his to claim. Right-mindedness

came from the Jains and most of his philosophy as well as the Dharma came from earlier sources. This leads to the belief that the Jains and Buddhists were at one time a part of Hindu Brahmanism and in Weber's *History of Indian Literature* the quazi-atheist element of Buddhism is seen as primordial and the Janis are actually regarded as early Buddhists. It was King Asoka who really promoted Buddhism about 250 BC, but there is too much evidence against the incredible amount of teachings accredited to Buddha to be disregarded.

And, too, there was animism before anything else. To try to study animism is an exercise in insanity. Besides that, to what purpose do we seek the truth when the truth is only within ourselves? Buddha had said that the truth is within all of us; it only takes the experiencing of it to make it real.

As Robertson says, both Jesus and Buddha became historical figures when that need of credibility arose in questioning minds. "Men who are taught to bow ethically to a divine teacher are not taught ethically, to think!"

I really like that and it bears repeating: "Men who are taught to bow ethically to a divine teacher are not taught ethically, to think!"

If we are to believe in these figures who demand our subservience, we should also admit to checking our brains at the door of the temple, church or synagogue.

In the end, remember that Mr. Robertson was a Western man who seems as cynical as only a Western man's mind can think. There is much more to the differences of the Eastern and Western thinking.

Why East or West?

MADAME BLAVATSKY FOUNDED A SOCIETY called the Theosophical Society. It claims the membership of many learned persons. In Theosophy one finds that mystical speculation is applied to deduce a philosophy of the universe. In its modern phase, it is a system that claims to embrace the essential truth underlying *all* systems of religion, science and philosophy. Its doctrines closely resemble those of Buddha and Brahmanism which teaches the existence of an omnipotent, infinite, eternal and immutable set of principles transcending the power of human conception and the identity of all souls, through the cycle of incarnation with a universal spirit.

I mention this because it would appear to be an intellectual effort to unify the thinking and bring the East and West closer together with the purpose of understanding. As man does not possess a soul in Buddhist belief, it would seem to be an uphill battle. It seems even less probable when one reads Donald Lopez, Jr. in the Foreword of *The Tibetan Book of Great Liberation* by W.Y. Evens-Wentz, a much respected scholar, translator and writer. He writes, "The undifferentiated dichotomy of the materialistic West and the mystic East, an East that holds the secret to the West's redemption" makes the two incompatible in purpose unless there is a total recapitulation by the West.

The repeated efforts by scholars to reconcile the East and the West have largely been a series of failures and make one wonder why one should try. Before Marco Polo philosophy and religion developed without intermingling, so what is the concern? Is it which one is right for mankind and why?

I suppose that if one is free to choose the issues, it becomes moot. The reconciliation or wars between the East and West have now redeveloped themselves from religion to the economics and materialism driving both sides of a political picture.

To the aforementioned Donald Lopez, Jr. the thought process of SEM: the Ordinary Mind brings us to focus on the East and West by saying, "Because it is undistinguishable, ordinary and remains where it is, the clear and lucid knowing is called, "the ordinary mind." No matter what auspicious and poetic names are used, it is, in fact, nothing other than the personal awareness. Whoever wants more is like someone searching for the elephant's tracks when the elephant has been found."

Carl G. Jung, the great intellect of human psychology, by invitation of the author W.Y. Evans-Wentz, wrote the psychological commentary for *The Tibetan Book of the Great Liberation*. His comments are vividly appropriate to the understanding of differences of Eastern and Western thought and the processes establishing conclusions. To some extent, it also explains the dichotomy of science and religion. In his commentary he states that *the modern interpretation of the mind has switched from something metaphysical to being a psychic function.* It has no connection with the primordial oneness of the concept of the Universal Mind. In other words, there is no psychological data proving that the mind can exert itself beyond its own properties.

We are still, however, led to believe or to put our faith in something that can't happen, i.e., knowing God. Thus science opposes religion.

We tend to "think" of the mind as an arbitrary thing, but

the truth is that every reality is a psychic image and nothing exists unless we are able to mentally see it. We are obsessed with conditions of factual structure and the clear and present danger is that unless we learn to think beyond that, we accept what others say and that becomes our perception.

In the East, the mind is cosmic and so there is no conflict between religion and science. As Carl Jung explains it, "There is no conflict between religion and science in the East because no science there is based upon the passion for facts, and no religion upon mere faith."

The East does not have a body of modern psychology as does the West. The East does have a vast reservoir of philosophy or metaphysics. Critical philosophy, as a precursor to psychology, therefore has no meaning in the East. However, cosmic philosopher Roderic Knowles comments that in that sense that psychology literally means, "Logic of the soul" the Eastern psychology has been vastly superior for centuries – especially when one considers that institutionalized modern psychology actually ignores the soul.

In the East, the word for "mind" has a definite metaphysical connotation whereas in the West the "mind" is a psychic function. We don't know what "psych" is, but can deal with the phenomenon of "mind" leaving us with the conclusion that psychology is a science of mere phenomenon without metaphysical implications or connections with the Universal Mind. Henceforth, the West became disconnected from the cosmos or world soul with the discovery of our psych – which most are convinced is a biochemical process within the brain cells.

I think we are, in the West, ignoring the damage ego causes because ego has become a psychological spectacle which is both revered and enforced by societal fraud. Witness our "stars" in every aspect of our lives.

So, WHAT WE PRIMARILY HAVE replacing us in the Universal Mind is a Western *Psychic Belch*. Not many regard or recognize the psychic phenomenon as a category of existence as such and it's the only category to which we have as access to immediate knowledge because nothing can be known without first appearing and becoming instantly verifiable as a psychic image.

The basic difference between the East and the West is that the West relies on the psych as its primary existence and the East has adopted the extraversional "style." East looks inward, West presses outward. The West looks upon the church for its salvation, the East believes in self-liberation. In the West we look at all events as being outside and the East all existence emanates from within.

Knowles would add to the argument against this, saying that slavish external referencing is as observable throughout the East as it is in the West.

At one point, Jung quotes Kierkegaard, saying, "Before God man is always wrong and by fear, repentance, promises, submission, self-abasement, good deeds and praise he perpetuates the great power which is not himself, but *totaliter aliter,* the Wholly Other, altogether perfect and 'outside,' the only reality."

The differences are still so vast between the East and the West that it is unlikely that a perfect understanding can take place. I think Jung argues that we are either Eastern or Western. The West uses ego; in the East, if there is no ego there is nobody to be conscious of anything and the Eastern mind can conceive of consciousness without an ego. In the practice of the higher forms of yoga, in striving to reach *Samadhi*, the ego becomes dissolved. Jung says, "We in the West believe that a truth is satisfactory only if it can be verified by external facts." In the East a far more subjective view prevails. Jung doubted the blessings of Western civilization and he has similar misgivings as to the adoption of Eastern spirituality by the West.

In our Western world man cannot accomplish his own redemption and it must come from the Western Christian viewpoint. In the East man has, for thousands of years, accomplished his own salvation because that is how you do it. Modern analytical psychology, a Western invention, is now leaning toward a process in the unconscious which can compensate for the defects of the conscious attitude, but for it to be successful the transformation is still tied to divine intervention. It would seem that there is a need for prayer to be recognized as the final healing factor.

As disparate as the two sides may be, Jung sees both sides as having psychological justification. Both attempt to overcome the "mere naturalness of life."

Jung also advises against getting involved in yoga unless you have made a careful analysis of the possible unconscious reaction and perhaps that is where I ventured too far. He also says, quite cryptically, "What is the use of initiating yoga if your dark side remains as good medieval Christian as ever? If you can afford to seat yourself on a gazelle skin under a Bo-tree or in the cell of a gommpa for the rest of your life without being troubled by politics or the collapse of your securities, I will look favorably upon your case. But yoga in Mayfair or Fifth Avenue, or any other place which is on the telephone, is a spiritual fake." From my personal experience, some of which have already been put forward, I would certainly agree. There seems to be something revoltingly chic about some modern pseudo practitioners – those who have their personal trainers, their personal meditation guides, their personal yoga instructors. It's just another ego trip and I abhor it. Candy-coated baloney is still baloney. There is an old movie maker's urging, "Cut to the chase," and in our short time on earth and in preparing for leaving it I think the term applies. There is no truth in ignorance, and it was in that ignorance that Buddha was held until he determined to sit under that Bo tree and meditate until he became enlightened. When he attained all knowledge he "awakened" and the world changed.

But, in the West, before truth there is conjecture, so the game is on and the game now is Higgs particle.

There is an enormous underground structure called the Large Hadron Collider. The cool society calls it LHC. It is 17 miles in circumference and it is located under the French–Swiss border.

The purpose of this mammoth circular particle accelerator is to crack the code of the physical world. Physicists have been able to build a Standard Model on the theory that everything around us is made of particles called quarks and leptons with four kinds of forces that influence the accepted as the building blocks of the universe.

The first of the three known forces are electromagnetism and gravity as one. The second is a strong force that binds atomic nuclei together and the third is a weak force, which causes nuclear reactions that have let the sun continue to shine for billions of years. Comparatively, it is good sized stuff.

The result of these forces, trillions of neutrinos from the sun go through our bodies every second without our ever feeling them because that weak force *is* so very weak.

The Standard Model cannot explain a number of great mysteries concerning the surrounding universe that are hidden in the miniscule paradigm of particles and forces. How is it that this now vast and unfathomable cosmos, this "universe" that we now see was once smaller than an atom?

By using the supercollider to smash pieces of matter together under conditions exactly duplicating, or more correctly, arrogantly claimed as those at one billionth of a second following the big bang, it is hoped the physicists can recover and study the theoretical Higgs particle or Higgs boson. It could be the missing fourth part of the building blocks they previously haven't been able to locate and measure.

The Higgs particle might be what gives the fundamental particles mass. This boson is thought to be huge when compared to many other subatomic particles. Joel Achenbach wrote that building a contraption like the supercollider to find the Higgs particle is a bit like embarking on a career as a stand-up comic with the hope that at some point you happen to blurt out a joke that's not only side-splittingly funny, but also a palindrome.

In a way, this has already happened. The Higgs boson was termed the God particle by Leon Lederman, who like Einstein, Rutherford, Max Planck, Niels Bohr and Werner Heisenberg before him, were not exactly stand-up comics.

Perhaps there is no need to find the fourth building block. The particle that's being sought which glues mass together is quite obviously in us, in our bodies and as such also constitutes the construct of the brain. It is present in Sem, the ordinary mind.

Behavioral science can be said to lack proven qualities as does the previously mentioned standard model. When a force mediating particle is exchanged at a macro level the effect is equivalent to a force influencing them both, and the particle is said to have *mediated* that force.

We are contained within our own collider. Our general behavior is governed by the chemical balance or imbalance as our bodily electrolytes spark our actions. The massive scalar elementary particle predicted to exist by the standard model could mediate naturally conducive fear which generates a sub-mental product known to all of us as religious belief.

In Buddhism we are taught there is no creator God. God is within all of us. It is also said that Buddha's enlightenment awakened him to all knowledge. He was ignorant of nothing. Is the Higgs particle in human mass actually the generator now called religion?

Up until now there are only indirect experimental indications for the existence of the Higgs boson, and it cannot be claimed to have been found. Nevertheless, there has been a good deal of theoretical experimental research done to try to determine whether this particle science can be extended into a complete theory of everything.

Thus far there is nothing substantive which can refute the factual determinant that our minds and bodies formally function in unison. *Incipient particle balance* can conceivably generate the electromagnetic impulses that govern our thought process and are inherent in our mental management. And, it is possible, the promotion of fear. And, our seemingly fundamental need for religion. Physics also tells us that, again, for every action there is an equal reaction. That being true, the reaction to fear is to seek protection or security, i.e., the founding of a general super-Mom; religion.

In both philosophy and physics there are those who agree that there, in the subatomic realm, is where physics and meta-physics meet. We have a good deal of deep thinking to do. While the answers are still up there or out there somewhere, we can do our best to overcome the ignorance imposed by traditional institutions and embrace humankind's ability to do so.

Quoting the philosopher Roderic Knowles once again, "It's our disconnectedness which is the root cause of our spiritual malaise and all other problems, whether planetary or personal – our disconnectedness from nature and the cosmos as living presence, as well as from the creative intelligence at work in nature and the cosmos, our disconnectedness from others, and above all, our disconnectedness with our innermost selves. Thus, first and foremost, we need to reconnect – which means going beyond the purely mental or intellectual, ever more fully into the experiential."

There is so much more to learn… No, no, no… not so much to learn… but rather, so much more to experience.

A GLOSSARY OF SORTS

A few terms and conditions might be helpful.

Padmasambhava said that the whole phenomenal Universe of appearances and *Nirvana* (the unmanifested or noumenal state) as an inseparable unity are in one's mind. (Meaning in its natural or unmodidified primordial state of Voidness).

Buddha: The *Nirvana* is a state of transcendence over that which is become born, made or formed. As such *Nirvana* is the annihilation of appearances.

Nagarjuna: Nothing can be said to exist or not to exist for as long as the mind conceives in terms of dualism, it is still under sangsaric bondage and fettered by the false desire for either personal immortality or annihilation. Reality is transcendent over both existence and non existence and over all other dualistic concepts.

At-one-ment: There being no duality, pluralism is untrue. There are no opposites — it is the same tree above and below. The opposites cancel each other, hence all is one.

<u>One Mind:</u> It is the unconscious. It is the eternal, unknown, not visible, not recognized, but it is also ever clear, ever existing, radiant and unobscured. The coming of the One Mind leads to the freedom of the Mind (or deliverance) which is the purpose of the *Dharma* through *Buddha* or *Hinduism*.

<u>Desires</u> crave external fulfillment which ties man to the world of consciousness. It is the gravest of weaknesses. Westerners, upon the discovery of the unconscious, sometimes pounce upon it with the same greed that they have for possessions. We cannot compel it; it has to come by its own accord and be accepted with grace and humility.

<u>Phenomenon</u> means something visible or directly observable, as an appearance, action change or occurrence of any kind as distinguished from the force by which, or the law in accordance with which, it may be produced.

<u>True Essence</u> embraces all phenomena and all things and beings exist in it and by it. There is no place in the universe where the Essentiality of a Buddha is not present. Far and wide throughout the spaces of space, the Buddha Essence is present and perpetually manifested.

<u>Universal Essence</u> is the One Mind. It is the source of all bliss of *Nirvana* and all sorrow is of the Sangsara.

<u>Mind,</u> in its microscopic aspect, is variously described by the unenlightened as soul or ego.

<u>The True State:</u> *Nirvana* as the Voidness, like the Sun, shines unceasingly. Man becomes nearly perfectly igno-

rant. *Nirvana* is empty of all conceivable things. We have
traveled a great distance away from the reunion of the part
with the whole. At some point, the teachers tell us we will
realize the folly of our ignorance (perhaps through many
rebirths) and choose Divine Wisdom and our return or pilgrimage returns us from the Other Shore.

Time and Space: In the True State of the Supra or Mundane
Mind, there is no time, just as there is no thing. With the
birth of the Cosmos, time is born and it stops with the end
of the Cosmos. Mind is the container of matter, and form
as of time and space. Therefore, there is no past, no present
and no future. There is, however, the condition of timelessness which is the unending present, and it is of an eternal
duration so when we talk about everything living in the
now, it simply means we are perpetual state of timelessness
with no past and no future. Past and future are miscon-
ceived dualities. In the True State time is beginningless
and endless and cannot be divided into the past, present and
future. So space is dimensionless, and divisionless, and non
existent apart from the One Mind or the Voidness.

When the mind attains the True State and is naked, the
world ceases to exist, so do time and space as they are of the
same illusory nature as is the mundanenss of mind. The
One Mind does not contain any thoughts as men know
thought. It contains all things, yet is no-thing. It comprises
existences, but has no existence. The human mind can, by
process of *yoga* attain ecstatic consciousness of its parental
source and become one with it in essence, but the human
microscopic mind, even though it has becomes a finite part
of the macro-mind, will never discover the Primary or
Secondary Cause. One must transcend human existence

to the state of the Clear Light of Reality and therefore, *sangsarically* cease to exist.

<u>Individualized and Collective Mind:</u> There is but one Cosmic Mind (There is but one sun, the days are countless).   All humans and subhuman creatures, like a single cell, collectively constitute the body of one multi-cellular organism, mentally illuminated by the One Cosmic Mind. Others and self are identical. Because of what Buddha calls ignorance we fail to live by the Golden Rule. Singularly we are weak and susceptible to *sansaric* repetition.

Similarly, individual ideas and functions benefit only a few, whereas Buddhahood makes us all one and serves to profit everything forever.

<u>Wisdom and Knowledge:</u> Worldly wisdom is born of worldly sense in their *sangsaric* aspect. Higher knowledge is hidden in men and needs *Dharma* awakening. The Kanjur lists Eight Treasures of Learning:

1. Ever-present, innate learning, like the One Mind is always there.
2. The treasure of *yogic* learning which develops the mundane mind.
3. The treasure of the *yogic* reflection and meditation.
4. The treasure of learning to be retained in the mind after having been heard or understood, sometimes as in our treatise in the form of *yogic* formulae.
5. The treasure of fortitude in learning.
6. The treasure of the secret, initial learning or knowledge of the Doctrine.
7. The treasure of the Bodhisattiva's saintly

heart, born of indomitable faith in the
Tri Kaya or Three Divine Bodies.

8. The treasure of the spiritual perfection acquired through listening to the Dharma
and meditation on the Dharma.

Wisdom dissipates the mists of illusion and Knowledge
nurtures it. Understanding the conscious or external
world is knowledge whereas it is the understanding called
Wisdom with which the mastery of the *yogi* is concerned.
It is in Wisdom, not in knowledge, that in future time man
will at last discover Right Law, Right Society and Right
Government.

Illiteracy and Utilitarianism: It is not necessary to attain
enlightenment. The knowledge of science has raped the
earth. Its main use may be in attaining material goods. It
would better serve to be seeking insight toward the Divine
Wisdom of the Supra-mundane and into True Reality, beyond the *Sangsara* in the True State. There may be a time
when man must forget all he has learned in order to rethink
his values.

Padmasambhava revisited: The Great Guru advocated
disregard for the common acceptances of right and wrong.
Good and evil and the repetition of trying to overcome the
dualism of good and evil leads to Tantricism where there is
neither this nor that, but at one-ment wherein there is transcendence over all opposites as well as over good and evil.

Tantric Buddhism: It is defined as a method of attaining
ecstatic union with the One Mind (Absolute Consciousness)
known as *yoga*, but according to W.Y. Evans-Wentz, "we

should, perhaps, be justified in defining Tantricism as being a school of eclectic esotericism, based fundamentally upon *yoga* practically applied, both to esoteric Brahmanism and to esoteric (Mahayana) Buddhism." (It should be pointed out that esotericism is that which has been adapted exclusively for the initiated or enlightened few, another case for philoso-religious supermen. Brahmanism is the religious and social system of the Brahmans. For both it means developed by the inner circle. There are both peaceful and wrathful gods, goddesses and lesser deities visualized but they best serve to (as said, "to practically") interpret human nature pragmatically.

Whether or not it is meant to warn and assure at the same time, it is meant primarily to teach the understanding, the sublimation, of reproduction. Birth is balanced by death. It teaches the science of sex and Padmasambhava was a great, near super practitioner.

<u>Astrology:</u> It is believed that man is integrally influenced by astrology, but it doesn't imply it is fatal because the *yoga* master is also the master of the heavenly seas. The astrological influences are to be recognized because they affect all growing and living creatures, both sentient and non-sentient.

The Yoga

ONE NEED NOT HAVE A GURU to practice, but they are helpful. We can practice without one. "When the disciple is ready, the master will appear."

The goal is the attainment of *Nirvana*. It is the *yogic* process of moving the mundane mind into the Supra-mundane Mind.

The first step is the study and understanding of Divine Wisdom. Second is the process to intuitional insight and the third disciple stands face to face with the Nakedness. If the breath is controlled, the mind is at rest or peace. Eating only vegetables increases the power of breath concentration. The meditation is on Truth and thoughts dismissed, then the "Who am I?", then the suppression of all thought. The Universe is centered in the mind. The mind is manifested through animal sensuousness, then all living organisms, or forms, independent of form and in its primordial, unmodified condition of nakedness. When the *sangsaric* mind is transcended, suffering will end. All *sangsaric* aspects are unreal and illusory. The essential purpose is *yogic understanding* of our own microscopic aspect of the mind so it will be realized in its true state as a part of the One Mind. Man must meditate to join the whole self as but one. "Without knowledge there is no meditation; without meditation there is no knowledge. He who hath both knowledge and meditation is near *Nirvana*." Buddha.

The Problem of Self

AM I REALLY SOMETHING? Is anything real or only *karmic* image? One should strive to understand all selves are one, the Self. By losing oneself one finds one's Self, the impersonalized self extinction. When one detaches oneself from attainment one can be delivered from the *sangsaric* bondage of ignorance and from wrong belief that appearances are real and that there is an immortal self. Once on that Path, one advances beyond self to the One Mind and Emancipation from ignorance and toward Buddhahood. You are quieted from *karmic* reaction.

Psychology and the Therapy

THE MORE CIVILIZED WE BECOME, the less we are able to understand ourselves. Our process of civilization is but an attractive shroud we cover our true Self with. The basic, illiterate man more often understands our True Self. *Yoga* is the older, more fruitful in terms of overcoming ignorance, than psychological applications. Through countless ages we have absorbed the *sangsaric* content of human failure to understand the agonies brought by greed and possessiveness. Plotinus said, in effect, thought itself does not think and in order to attain the balanced state of one-ness one must practice without drawing within oneself to analyze oneself. "Know thyself!"

Knowles would say, "Experience your Self!"

Bardo Thodol

YOGIC TREATISES concerning various methods of attaining transcendence over ignorance. There are 16 of the treatises.

Conclusion

IT IS, IN THE END, senseless to spend one's life and health in pursuit of worldly goods. Life is short as well as uncertain and rather than waste it entirely we should try to do some good. Right View, Right Livelihood, Right Recollection, Right Endeavor, Right Meditation, Right Speech, Right Intentions and Right Judgment are all the right signposts.

Let those be our guide.

On the Western side of The One, as Plotinus describes it and his translators portray it, it is similar to enlightenment in unity, power and it is beyond the single mind. All later principles are subsequent to it. Discovery, knowledge and understanding stem from The One. It is all there within The One and it is the source of all human intelligence. Power emanates coincidentally with and from The One. It is a reservoir of the concept of all things, both natural and spiritual. It exists and always has existed; waiting to be discovered... *through the experiencing.* We draw from it and it never changes or decreases.

I liken it to Truth.

Lightning Source UK Ltd.
Milton Keynes UK
22 September 2010

160204UK00002B/8/P

9 780971 269354